CONCISE ANIMAL SCIENCE REFRESHER

Authors

Dr. Prasanta Kumar K Mishra, Dr. Anupama Jena,
Dr. Sadhna Ojha and Dr. Jatin Kumar Sahoo

AkiNik Publications
New Delhi

Published By: *AkiNik Publications*

AkiNik Publications
169, C-11, Sector - 3,
Rohini, Delhi-110085, India
Toll Free (India) – 18001234070

Author: *Dr. Prasanta Kumar K Mishra, Dr. Anupama Jena, Dr. Sadhna Ojha and Dr. Jatin Kumar Sahoo*

1st Edition: *2018*

Pages: *168*

ISBN: *978-93-88112-85-7*

Price: *₹ 765/-*

Preface

This book is being compiled considering the needs of B.V.Sc. and A.H. undergraduate students. Animal science comprises of a vast syllabus but compared to that test or MCQ books available are few in numbers. The idea to give students a short, concise but useful review lead to the inception of this manuscript. We expect that student will be benefited from this book.

I would like to thanks the co-authors of this book Dr Anupama, Dr Sadhna, Dr Jatin, Dr Anil and Dr. Indhu for their constant efforts and suggestions during compilation of this books.

On behalf of the team, I would further like to extend our humble gratitude to our teachers during UG, PG and PhD who have directly or indirectly paved the way to science by creating urge for knowledge among us.

Finally, I would like to thank AkiNik publisher for their support and help in publishing this book

May God Bless all

Dr. Prasanta Kumar K Mishra

IVRI

About the Book

This book gives an overview of all the subjects included in animal science. Students read many of the text books but while preparing for any entrance examination they miss some key points, what they supposed to know, as the question setter tries to distinguish between students by asking questions from those missed portions. So, in this book we have tried to cover all the units in every subject by referring many text books, while emphasizing the most probable questions. By referring these questions students will definitely get an idea of types of questions being set in different entrance examinations so also will get an idea how to prepare for the exam. Though it was very much difficult to concise all the subjects of animal science within this limited number of questions but we tried best to give the students the idea how to pick the questions from the text and memorize that for different examinations like ICAR-JRF, SRF, NET etc.

Any suggestion to improve the book or any comment on the book are welcomed. One can write to us about that.

Thank you and wish you best for upcoming examinations.....

Content

Chapter - 1

Veterinary Biochemistry

Dr. Prasanta Kumar K Mishra and Dr. Anil Gattani

1) **The First Enzyme to be Isolated Was**
   a) Lipase
   b) Zymase
   c) Urease
   d) Revertase
2) **Enzymes are Classified Into.......Different Classes**
   a) 4
   b) 6
   c) 5
   d) 8
3) **Aldolase are Example of......**
   a) Ligase
   b) Oxidoreductase
   c) Isomerase
   d) lyases
4) **ATP is Exclusively Required for**
   a) Ligases
   b) Oxidoreductase
   c) Isomerase
   d) lyases
5) **Functional Unit of Enzyme is Known as**
   a) Holoenzyme
   b) Apoenzyme
   c) Co-factor
   d) Prosthetic group

6) **Tightly Bound Organic Non-Protein Groups to Enzymes are Known as**

a) Prosthetic groups

b) Ligands

c) Co-factor

d) Modulator

7) **Km is Defined by**

a) Enzyme concentration

b) Substrate concentration

c) Co factor concentration

d) Product concentration

8) **Low Km Indicates**

a) Enzyme has less affinity to substrate

b) Substrate concentration is very high

c) Higher affinity of enzyme

d) Reaction is irreversible

9) **Double Reciprocal Plot (Lineweaver-Burk) is Important in**

a) Enzyme inhibition

b) Enzyme coagulation

c) Enzyme immobilisation

d) Substrate localization

10) **Xanthine Oxidase and Enolase Contains.....and.......as Co-Factors**

a) Mo and Fe

b) Fe and Ca

c) Mo and Cu

d) Mo and Mg

11) **Enzymes**

a) Increase velocity of reaction

b) Change equilibration of reaction

c) Increase activation energy

d) Are always protein

12) Most Frequently Found Amino Acids Near Active Site Of An Enzyme Are

a) Lys and Ser
b) Ser and Tyr
c) Phe and Gly
d) Thr and Pro

13) In Competitive Type of Enzyme Inhibition Km Value.... Whereas Vmax....

a) Both remains constant
b) Km increases but Vmax remain constant
c) Both increases
d) Km decreases but v max remains constant

14) In Non-Competitive Enzyme Inhibition Vmax and Km

a) Km is constant but Vmax decreases
b) Vmax and Km both decreases
c) No effect
d) Both increases

15) Enhancement of Enzyme Inhibition by Binding to the Enzyme is Categorised Under

a) Competitive inhibition
b) Non-competitive Inhibition
c) Suicidal inhibition
d) Enhancer inhibition

16) Co Enzymes are

a) Organic but non protein in nature
b) Can be metal ions
c) Always derived from vitamins
d) all of the above

17) Allosteric Effectors Bind to the.....Site of Enzymes

a) Active site
b) Activator site
c) Allosteric site
d) Modulation site

18) Velocity of Allosteric Enzyme Versus Substrate Concentration Gives

a) Sigmoidal curve

b) Hyperbolic curve

c) Straight line

d) Bell shaped curve

19) Effect of Temperature and pH Upon Enzyme Results in

a) Oval curve

b) Bell shaped structure

c) Rectangular curve

d) Liner curve

20) Inhibition of First Step by the Product in a Multi-Step Reaction is Known as

a) Feedback inhibition

b) Allosteric inhibition

c) Suicidal inhibition

d) Heterotropic inhibition

21) Enzyme Units Can be Represented in

a) Katal

b) IU

c) Somogyi

d) all of the above

22) Ribozymes are

a) Not enzymes

b) Enzymes with ribitol

c) Made up of RNA

d) Non catalytic

23) Streptokinase are

a) Used in removal of blood clots

b) Available commercially

c) Also known as urokinase

d) All of the above

24) Isoenzymes are

a) Of similar molecular weight
b) Catalyses same reaction
c) They have same Km
d) All of the above

25) LDH Has..... Isoenzymes

a) 7
b) 5
c) 4
d) 2

26) LDH_1 is Specific for Disturbances Related to ......whereas LDH5 is Specific for...

a) Heart and brain
b) Heart and muscle/liver
c) Heart and kidney
d) Brain and liver

27) Elevated Creatine Phosphokinase 2 is Indicator of Disorders Related to

a) Muscle
b) Heart
c) Kidney
d) Brain

28) Alkaline Phosphatase is Increased in

a) Bone diseases
b) Brain diseases
c) Bile diseases
d) Behavioural diseases

29) PSA is an Indicator in

a) Pancreatic cancer
b) Prostate cancer
c) Pagets disease
d) Porcine syndrome

30) Van Den Bergh Indirect and Direct Positive are Indicator of

a) Haemolytic and mixed type of jaundice

b) Obstructive and hepatic jaundice

c) Obstructive type jaundice

d) Haemolytic and obstructive type

31) AST/SGPT are Specific Indicator for

a) Liver damages

b) Liver damages in ruminants

c) Kidney damage

d) Gall bladder damage

32) AST/ALT Ratio is Normally

a) 1

b) 0.6

c) 0.8

d) 0.2

33) In Hepatic Jaundice Serum Conjugated Bilirubin Concentration....

a) Increases

b) Decreases

c) Not affected

d) Not significant

34) Hepatic Jaundice is Characterized by

a) Increased serum unconjugated bilirubin

b) Increased excretion of urobilinogen

c) Both a and b

d) None of the above

35) ......is an Positive Acute Phase Protein

a) C Reactive Protein

b) Albumin

c) RBP

d) Transferrin

36) Glomerular Filtration Rate (GFR) is Measured by

a) Inulin
b) PAH
c) Creatinine
d) Albumin

37) A Protein used in Kidney Function Test is

a) C Reactive Protein
b) Albumin
c) Cystatin C
d) Transferrin

38) Elevated Plasma Bicarbonate Concentration Just after Meal is Known as

a) Acidic tide
b) Acidity
c) Alkaline tide
d) Alkalosis

39) Ketosis Can be Diagnosed from

a) Nitroprusside reaction
b) Kohler reaction
c) Rose bengal plate test
d) Nessler reaction

40) GODPOD Method is Mostly Used for Estimation of

a) Serum urea
b) Blood glucose
c) Blood pH
d) Serum creatinine

41) Movement of Solvent Through SPM to Concentrated Solution is Known as

a) Osmosis
b) Diffusion
c) Migration
d) Brownian movement

42) Separation of a Mixture of Chemical Can be Achieved by

a) Electrophoresis
b) Chromatography
c) Centrifugation
d) osmosis

43) Migration of Charged Particle under an Electric Field is Known as

a) Electrophoresis
b) Reverse osmosis
c) Chromatography
d) None of the above

44) Agarose Gel Electrophoresis is Used for Analysis of.........

a) Nucleic acid
b) Protein
c) Lipids
d) Carbohydrates

45) Lipids can be Easily Detected and Quantified by.

a) TLC
b) GC-MS
c) HPLC
d) All of the above

46) Protein Sequencing can be Done by

a) Dinitro benzene
b) Mass spectrometry
c) Edman's reagent
d) All of the above

47) SDS-PAGE is Used for Mostly

a) Protein
b) Carbohydrate
c) Lipids
d) steroids

48) Colorimetry Deals with….. And Spectrophotometry with…..

a) Single wavelength and multiple wavelength

b) Both single wavelength

c) Both multiple wavelength

d) All of the above

49) Flame Photometry is used for

a) Turbidity

b) Electrolytes

c) Protein sample

d) Bacterial culture

50) Tritium has Half-Life of

a) 12 hours

b) 12 years

c) 15 seconds

d) 10 days

51) Vitamers are

a) Chemically similar to vitamin

b) Similar activity to vitamin

c) Alcohol or aldehyde derivatives of vitamins

d) All of the above

52) β Carotene is also Known as… and Gives … Retinal Molecules upon Hydrolysis

a) Pro vitamin A, 2

b) Plant vitamin A, 2

c) Retinoic acid, 1

d) Retinal, 5

53) The Sun Shine Vitamin D has Precursor as

a) 7-dehydrocholestrol

b) Pregnanolone

c) Arachidonate

d) Prostaglandin

54) Hydroxylation Sites for 1,25 Position in Vitamin D3 are

a) Liver and kidney

b) Kidney

c) Kidney and liver

d) Liver

55) Which among the Tocol Ring Derived Vitamin E Isomer is Most Potent in Nature

a) Alpha tocopherol

b) Beta tocopherol

c) Gamma tocopherol

d) Delta tocopherol

56) Selenium has Sparing Action on

a) Vit-A

b) Vit-B1

c) Vit-E

d) Vit-D3

57) Synthetic form of Vitamin K is Known as

a) Menaquinone

b) Menadione

c) Naphthoquinone

d) Selenedione

58) Deficiency of Enzyme Gulonolactone Oxidase Impairs Formation of Vitamin

a) A

b) D

c) C

d) K

59) Thiamine Pyrophosphate is Essential in

a) Transketolase reaction

b) Dehydrogenase mediated reactions

c) BERI beri

d) All of the above

60) Deficiency of Vitamin B2 Results in

a) Glossitis
b) Dermatitis
c) Cheilosis
d) All of the above

61) Tryptophan can be Given in Pellagra to Compensate for Which Vitamin

a) B2
b) B5
c) Niacin
d) B6

62) Vitamin Involved in Transamination and Deamination Reactions is

a) B6
b) B3
c) B9
d) B7

63) Biotin is used as Co-Enzyme in

a) Carboxylation
b) Transulfuration
c) Methylation
d) Ribosylation

64) Folic Acid is

a) Pteroglutamic acid
b) Involved in one carbon atom metabolism
c) Derived from green leafy vegetables
d) All of the above

65) Deficiency of Vitamin B12 May Lead to

a) Pernicious anaemia
b) Megaloblastic anaemia
c) Methyl malonyl aciduria
d) Both a and c

66) **Insulin has ....Chains with Total ...Amino Acids**

a) 2, 54

b) 3, 51

c) 3, 56

d) 2, 51

67) **Deficiency of Growth Hormone can Cause ..... And Overproduction May Cause.....**

a) Dwarfism and tallish

b) Dwarfism and acromegaly/gigantism

c) Cretinism and acromegaly/gigantism

d) None of the above

68) **Hyperthyroidism May Lead to..... But Hypothyroidism Causes.....**

a) Grave's disease and dwarfism

b) Cretinism or Grave's disease

c) Grave's disease and Cretinism

d) None of the above

69) **Addison's Disease is Due to ....and Cushing's Syndrome is Due to.....**

a) Hypo and hyper adrenocorticism

b) Hypo and hyper thyroidism

c) Both of the above

d) None of the above

70) **Parent Structure of Steroidal Hormone is**

a) Pregnanolone

b) Cholesterol

c) Cortisol

d) None of the above

71) **Testosterone to DHT Conversion is Mediated by**

a) 5-α- reductase

b) Aromatse

c) Hydroxylase

d) None of the above

72) Insulin is Released by

a) Stimulation from glucose

b) Stimulation from arginine and leucin

c) Secretin

d) All of the above

73) Half-Life of Insulin in Plasma is

a) 5 minutes

b) 2 minutes

c) 1 hour

d) 67 days

74) Glucagon Exhibits its Activity Via

a) Insulin

b) cGMP

c) cAMP

d) None of the above

75) Epinephrine ....Blood Glucose Level

a) Decreases

b) Increases

c) Does not affect

d) Causes pulsatile release of

76) Simplest Monosaccharide is

a) Glyceral dehyde

b) Glucose

c) Fructose

d) Trehalose

77) Enantiomers are

a) Mirror images

b) Designated as D/L

c) D type are more prevalent

d) All of the above

78) Non-Mirror Stereoisomers are

a) Anomers
b) Epimers
c) Diastereoisomers
d) Tautomers

79) Fructose has a Specific Optical Rotation of

a) -92°
b) -62°
c) -98°
d) -56°

80) Benedict's test Exploits the

a) Reducing properties of sugar
b) Free OH group
c) Free S if any
d) Non reducing nature of sugar

81) Phenylhydrazine + Acetic Acid + Reducing Sugar (Δ)-----------

a) Formazone
b) Osazone
c) Ozone
d) Oxygen

82) Blood Group Antigen Contains--------- Sugar

a) Fucose
b) Rhamnose
c) Sucrose
d) Maltose

83) Sucrose is a ---------Type of Sugar

a) Reducing
b) Non-reducing
c) Activating
d) Inactivating

84) Lactose is a Disaccharide with β.....Linkage

a) 1-4

b) 1-2

c) 1-6

d) 1-1

85) Starch Contains---------- and---------------- Percentage of Amylose and Amylopectin

a) 20 and 80

b) 12 and 88

c) 50/50

d) 40 and 60

86) Hydrolysis of Cellulose forms

a) Starch

b) Glycogen

c) Cellobiose

d) None of the above

87) Glycosaminoglycans are Formed from

a) Amino sugars + lipid

b) Uronic acid + amino sugars

c) Protein + sugars

d) All of the above

88) Which of the GAG Does not Contain any Uronic Acid

a) Chondroitin sulphate

b) Heparin

c) Dermatan sulphate

d) Kearatan sulfate

89) Hexokinase and Pyruvate Kinase Catalyses.... Steps of Glycolysis

a) Reducing

b) Reversible

c) Irreversible

d) None of the above

90) which Step of Glycolysis is Rate Limiting in Nature

a) PFK mediated
b) Hexokinase
c) Pyruvate kinase
d) PT isomerase

91) TCA Cycle is Negatively Regulated by

a) ATP
b) Succinyl Co-A
c) NADH
d) All of the above

92) How Many ATPs are Generated in Kreb's Cycle

a) 18
b) 12
c) 5
d) 1

93) PEP Carboxykinase is an Important Enzyme in

a) Glycolysis
b) Gluconeogenesis
c) Lipolysis
d) None of the above

94) Glycogen Synthesis Requires a Primer as

a) Glycogenin
b) Saponin
c) Tannin
d) RNA

95) Pentose Phosphate Pathway is Essential as

a) NADPH generation
b) Ribose cycling
c) Both a and b
d) None

96) Von Gierke's Disease is Due to Deficiency of

a) Glu-6- phosphatase

b) Hexokinase

c) PFK

d) A-1,4 glucosidase

97) Pompe's Disease is Due to the Deficiency of

a) Glu-6- phosphatase

b) Hexokinase

c) PFK

d) A-1,4 glucosidase

98) Glyoxylate Cycle Occurs in

a) Glyoxysome

b) Plants

c) Bacteria

d) All of the above

99) Complete Oxidation of 1 Mole of Glucose can Generate-------ATPs

a) 45

b) 38

c) 30

d) 10

100) Cori's Cycle Involves Conversion of--------- To Glucose in Liver

a) Pyruvate

b) Lactate

c) Alanine

d) All of the above

101) Esters of Fatty Acids with Alcohol are Known as

a) Simple lipids

b) Cholesterols

c) Fatty alcohol

d) All of the above

102) Nonessential Fatty Acid is

a) Linolenic

b) Oleic acid

c) Arachidonic acid

d) Linoleic acid

103) ω-3 Fatty Acid and ω-6 Fatty Acid are

a) Linolenic and linoleic

b) Arachidonic and linoleic

c) Linolenic and oleic acid

d) All of the above

104) Naturally Occurring Fatty Acids (PUFA) are.... Isomers

a) L-

b) D-

c) Trans

d) Cis

105) Plasmalogens Contain----- Linkages

a) Ester

b) Ethereal

c) Glycosidic

d) All of the above

106) Ceramide is the Parental Compound for

a) Sphingomyelin

b) Phosphatidic acids

c) None of the above

d) PE

107) Cerebrosides are Simplest

a) Glycolipids

b) Lipids

c) Fatty acids

d) PUFA

108) Iodine Number Indicates

a) Unsaturation in lipids
b) Saturation
c) Rancidity
d) All of the above

109) Reichert Meissl Number is Indicative of

a) Purity of lard
b) Purity of butter
c) Purity of cream
d) All of the above

110) Hydrolysis of Triacyl Glycerol by Alkali is Known as

a) Limefication
b) Saponification
c) Reduction
d) All of the above

111) β-oxidation of Fatty Acids Occurs in

a) Mitochondria
b) Lysosome
c) Peroxisome
d) All of the above

112) Zellweger Syndrome is Due to Absence of

a) Mitochondria
b) Peroxisome
c) Lysosome
d) Ribosomes

113) Net ATP Produced Upon Oxidation of One Mole of Palmitoyl co-A are

a) 132
b) 129
c) 88
d) Depend upon site of oxidation

114) Rate Limiting Enzyme in Ketogenesis is

a) Thiolase
b) HMG co-A synthase
c) Lyase
d) All of the above

115) Committed Step in Fatty Acid Synthesis is Catalysed by

a) Acetyl co-A carboxylase
b) FA synthase
c) None of the above
d) Both a and b

116) How many Essential Basic Amino Acids are There

a) 4
b) 3
c) 2
d) None

117) At Iso-Electric pH Protein Bears ...

a) No net charge
b) Charge
c) -ve charge
d) Both a and b

118) Zwitterions are

a) Hybrid ions
b) Both positive and negative charge bearing species
c) Dipolar ion
d) All of the above

119) Semi Essential Amino Acids are

a) Arg and Glu
b) Arg and lys
c) Arg and His
d) all of the above

120) Protein can be Termed to the Polypeptide with more than

a) 10
b) 50
c) 5
d) 34

121) Peptide Bonds are

a) Co valent
b) Rigid
c) Plannar
d) All of the above

122) Alpha Helix and Beta Sheets are Pertained to--------- Structure

a) Primary
b) Secondary
c) Tertiary
d) All of the above

123) Domains, the Units of Protein are a Part of

a) Primary
b) Secondary
c) Tertiary
d) Quaternary

124) Biuret Reaction Detects

a) Peptide bond
b) Two peptide bonds minimum
c) Dipeptide
d) All of the above

125) Sakaguchi and Millons Tests are for

a) Arg and Try
b) Try and Tyr
c) Tyr and Arg
d) Phe and His

126) Absorbance of Protein is Recorded at--------- nm Generally

a) 276

b) 210

c) 256

d) 280

127) Protamine and Histones are----- in Nature

a) Basic

b) Acidic

c) Neutral

d) Highly acidic

128) Purines are Numbered in ……Whereas Pyrimidines in……….

a) Serially, constantly

b) Anti-clock wise and clock wise

c) Clock wise and anti-clock wise

d) All of the above

129) Pentoses are bound to Nitrogenous Base by….. Bond in Nucleic Acids

a) β-N glycosidic bond

b) ω-N glycosidic bond

c) Phsopho diester bond

d) Ether bond

130) 1 bp of DNA Has a Molecular Weight of………..

a) 660 Da

b) 660 kDa

c) 330 Da

d) 330 kDa

131) RNA can be Identified by……. Staining

a) Orcinol

b) Resorcinol

c) Biuret

d) Lipocol

132) Most Abundant RNA Molecule are

a) t RNA
b) m RNA
c) r RNA
d) mi RNA

133) ------Is a Shunt Between Krebs Cycle and Urea Cycle

a) Fumarate
b) Arginosuccinate
c) Aspartate
d) Ornithine

134) Carbamoyl Phosphate Synthase I is the Rate Limiting Enzyme in-------

a) DNA synthesis
b) Purine synthesis
c) Pyrimidine synthesis
d) Urea cycle

135) Conversion of Phenyl Alanine to-------- Tyrosine is Mediated by

a) Phenyl alanine hydroxylase
b) Phenyl alanine oxidase
c) Phenyl alanine reductase
d) All of the above

136) During Phenyl Ketonuria----- is the Abnormal Constituent Excreted in Urine

a) Phenyl alanine
b) Phenyl pyruvate
c) Phenyl carbonate
d) none

137) Key Enzyme in Pathogenesis of Alkaptonuria is

a) Phenyl alanine hydroxylase
b) Phenyl alanine oxidase
c) Homogentisate oxidase
d) Homogentisate reductase.

138) Maple Syrup Urine Disease is Due to Deficiency of….. Enzyme.

a) Branched chain alpha keto acid dehydrogenase
b) Alpha keto acid transaminase
c) Alpha keto acid transferase
d) None

139) Which of the following is Ketogenic Amino Acids

a) Phenyl alanine
b) Alanine
c) Lysine
d) Methionine

140) The C4, 5 and N7 of Purine Nucleus is contributed by Amino Acid…

a) Phenyl alanine
b) Glycine
c) Lysine
d) Methionine

141) The end Product of Purine Metabolism is

a) Uric acid
b) Hypoxanthine
c) Allantoic acid
d) Varies as per species

142) HGPRT Deficiency of Purine Synthesis (Salvage Pathway) Results in

a) Gout
b) Anaemia
c) Lesch-Nyhan syndrome
d) Alzheimer's

Answer

1.c, 2.b, 3.d, 4.a, 5.a, 6.a, 7.b, 8.c, 9.a, 10.d, 11.a, 12.a, 13.b, 14.a, 15.c, 16.a, 17.c, 18.a, 19.b, 20.a, 21.d, 22.c, 23.d, 24.b, 25.b, 26.b, 27.b, 28.a, 29.b, 30.d, 31.a, 32.c, 33.a, 34.c, 35.a, 36.a, 37.c, 38.c, 39.a, 40.b, 41.a, 42.b, 43.a, 44.a, 45.d, 46.d, 47.a, 48.a, 49.b, 50.b, 51.d, 52.a, 53.a, 54.a, 55.a, 56.c, 57.b, 58.c, 59.d, 60.d, 61.c, 62.a, 63.a, 64.d, 65.a, 66.d, 67.b, 68.c, 69.a, 70.a, 71.a, 72.d, 73.a, 74.c, 75.b, 76.a, 77.d, 78.c, 79.a, 80.a, 81.b, 82.a, 83.b, 84.a, 85.a, 86.c, 87.b, 88.d, 89.c, 90.a, 91.d, 92.b, 93.b, 94.a, 95.c, 96.a, 97.d, 98.d, 99.b, 100.d, 101.a, 102.b, 103.a, 104.d, 105.b, 106.a, 107.a, 108.a, 109.b, 110.b, 111.a, 112.b, 113.b, 114.b, 115.a, 116.b, 117.d, 118.d, 119.c, 120.b, 121.d, 122.b, 123.c, 124.b, 125.b, 126.d, 127.a, 128.b, 129.a, 130.a, 131.a, 132.c, 133.a, 134.d, 135.a, 136.b, 137.c, 138.a, 139.c, 140.b, 141.d, 142.c.

Chapter - 2

Veterinary Biotechnology

Dr. Prasanta Kumar K Mishra and Dr. Indhu MS

1) **Introduction of Foreign DNA into Host Genetic Material is known as**
   a) Cloning of gene
   b) Insertion
   c) Incorporation
   d) None of the above
2) **Vectors are.......**
   a) Ds DNA
   b) Circular
   c) Covalently closed
   d) All of the above
3) **Plasmid can Carry up to Insert of Size**
   a) 10-20 kb
   b) 100 kb
   c) 200 kb
   d) 300 kb
4) **BAC are used for**
   a) Cloning sequence up to 300kb
   b) For generation of library
   c) For shotgun sequencing
   d) All of the above
5) **Cen Sequences are Present in**
   a) Plasmid
   b) BAC
   c) YAC
   d) PAC

6) **Restriction Enzymes Recognizes….**

a) Mirror repeats
b) Palindromic sequences
c) Inverted sequences
d) None

7) **Which Type of RE are Preferred for Gene Cloning Experiment**

a) Type I
b) Type III
c) Type II
d) All

8) ***EcoRI* recognises.**

a) Gaattc
b) Aagctt
c) Ggcc
d) Gcgc

9) **Primary Culture are**

a) The first passage cells
b) Derive directly from source
c) Are similar to the host genotype
d) All

10) **Trypsin is used at….. % Mostly in cell Culture Experiment**

a) 0.87
b) 0.25
c) 0.11
d) 0.35

11) **HEPES Buffer does not Require a Source of**

a) Bi-carbonate
b) Oxygen
c) Serum
d) Growth hormones

12) Serum is used typically at…….. % for Cell Culture

a) 5

b) 10

c) 20

d) 35

13) RPMI-1640 is Media used for Mostly

a) Fibroblast culture

b) Suspension culture

c) Tissue culture

d) Organ culture

14) PCR was Invented by Kary Mullis in

a) 1975

b) 1983

c) 1945

d) 1995

15) ………..Enzyme is a Common PCR Amplifier

a) Taq Polymerase

b) PFU Polymerase

c) Ligase

d) Lambda polymerase

16) Primers used in PCR are of Length

a) 18-30nt

b) 10-15nt

c) 50-100nt

d) 200nt

17) In PCR Amplification is

a) Linear

b) Cyclical

c) Exponential

d) Both a and c

18) Sensitivity of PCR is Normally

a) Pico-gram

b) Nano-gram

c) Micro-gram

d) gram

19) RFLP/VNTR/STR are used for

a) DNA fingerprinting

b) Restriction mapping

c) Loci determination

d) All of the above

20) *in-situ* Detection of Antigen can be Done by

a) FISH

b) Southern blot

c) Ligand trapping

d) Not possible

21) Southern Blot Deals with...... Whereas Northern Blot with.......

a) DNA and lipid

b) RNA and lipid

c) DNA and protein

d) DNA and RNA

22) Hybridisation of Nucleic Acid Needs a Probe of Length

a) 10-20

b) 30-40

c) 20-25

d) 8-19

23) CRISPR CAS9 is Used in

a) Mutant creation

b) Protein purification

c) RNA isolation

d) Enzyme estimation

24) Dolly was Created by

a) Somatic cell cloning

b) Gametic cloning

c) Hand guided cloning

d) All

25) Replication Length Shortening of Chromosomal ends are Refilled by

a) Telomerases

b) Replicases

c) Polymerases

d) Transcriptase

26) Insertion of Purine in the Place of Pyrimidine is Known as

a) Transition

b) Inversion

c) Transversion

d) None

27) Lac Operon is Example of

a) Constitutive expression

b) Repressible

c) Inducible operon

d) Fusion operon

28) Tryptophan Acts as...... in Trp Operon Whereas Allolactose as..... for Lac Operon

a) Repressor and inducer

b) Inducer and repressor

c) Inhibitor

d) Activator

29) Xeroderma Pigmentosum is Due to Disturbances in....... DNA Repair System

a) BER

b) NER

c) Both

d) None

30) Ethidium Bromide is used for Detection of

a) DNA

b) Protein

c) Lipid

d) Carbohydrate

31) What is the Need of Eukaryotic Protein Expression in Eukaryotic Host?

a) Protein folding

b) Post translational modification

c) Less antigenic

d) All of the above

32) Green Fluorescent Proteins are Mostly used as.... Tag

a) Silencer

b) Reporter

c) Activator

d) All

33) Ligation of DNA Sequences can be Done by

a) Sequanase

b) Synthase

c) T4 DNA ligase

d) Lyases

34) First DNA Polymerase was Isolated by

a) Tuniberg

b) Kornberg

c) Watson

d) Khurana

35) Fusion Agent in Hybridoma Production is

a) PEG

b) Sendai virus

c) Electric shock

d) All of the above

36) Monoclonal Antibodies are Specific for

a) Single virus
b) Single antigen
c) Single epitope
d) All

37) Larger DNA (more than 20 kb) are Electrophoresed in

a) PAGE
b) PFGE
c) CCE
d) 2D

38) Klenow Fragment Does not Have

a) Exonuclease activity
b) Proof reading activity
c) Polymerase activity
d) None

39) cDNA Library is....... Than Genomic Library

a) Smaller
b) Larger
c) Similar
d) None

40) Western Blotting Can Utilize

a) Antibody
b) Fluorescence
c) Chemiluminescence
d) all

41) DNA Synthesis is

a) Unidirectional
b) Bidirectional
c) Nondirectional
d) Multidirectional

42) Proofreading Activity to Maintain the Fidelity of DNA Synthesis

a) Occurs after the synthesis has been completed

b) Is a function of the 3'-5' exonuclease activity of the DNA polymerases

c) Requires the presence of an enzyme separate from the DNA polymerases

d) Occurs in prokaryotes but not eukaryotes

43) DNA Replicates through What Process?

a) Semi-conservative replication

b) Dispersive replication

c) Conservative replication

d) Disparative replication

44) DNA Helicase is found where?

a) Replication bubble

b) Replication Fork

c) Replication complex

d) All of these

45) Which of the Following has 5'-3' Exonuclease Activity?

a) DNA polymerase I

b) DNA polymerase II

c) DNA ligase

d) DNA Polymerase III

46) The Synthesis of DNA by DNA polymerase?

a) 3'-5' direction

b) 5'-5' direction

c) 5'-3' direction

d) 3'-3' direction

47) DNA Gyrase is Inhibited by

a) Tetracycline

b) Nalidixic acid

c) Cephalosporin

d) Both (a) and (b)

48) The Replicative Polymerase in *E. coli* is

a) DNA polymerase I

b) DNA polymerase II

c) DNA polymerase III

d) DNA polymerase IV

49) T_4 DNA Ligase

a) Requires ATP

b) Joins single-stranded DNA

c) Joins double-stranded DNA fragments with an adjacent 3'-phosphate and 5'-H

d) Requires NADH

50) The Klenow Fragment of *E. coli* Contains Which of the Following Activity?

a) Polymerase activity and proof reading activity

b) Polymerase activity and nick translation activity

c) Reverse transcriptase activity and nick translation activity

d) 5'-3' exonuclease activity

51) In Prokaryotes, the Lagging Primers are Removed by

a) 3'-5' exonuclease

b) DNA ligase DNA

c) Polymerase I

d) DNA polymerase III

52) Most of the Mistakes During DNA Replication are Corrected by

a) DNA ligase

b) DNA polymerase

c) Gyrase

d) helicase

53) The Specific Chromosomal Locations From Where the Replication Begins are Called as

a) Locus

b) Origin of replication

c) Loci

d) Chromosomal arms

54) The Synthesis That Proceeds in The Direction of the Replication Fork is the

a) Leading strand
b) Lagging strand
c) Parent strand
d) Neutral strand

55) Protein Which is Responsible for Keeping the DNA Unwound after Unwinding is

a) SSB proteins
b) SSC proteins
c) SSA proteins
d) SSD proteins

56) Newly Synthesized DNA Contains

a) Both new strands
b) Both old strand
c) One new and one old strand
d) Only one strand

57) The Main Enzyme to Polymerize Leading Strand of Eukaryotic DNA is

a) DNA polymerase α
b) DNA polymerase β
c) DNA polymerase γ
d) DNA polymerase δ

58) Which Enzyme Removes the RNA Primer During Replication?

a) RNA primase
b) DNA polymerase I
c) DNA ligase
d) Helicase

59) What is the Function of Helicase?

a) It forms bonds between DNA nucleotides
b) It adds new nucleotides to the DNA helix.
c) It forms the DNA helix
d) It separates DNA strands

60) Which of the Following Mechanisms will Remove Uracil and Incorporate the Correct Base?

a) Direct repair

b) Base excision repair

c) Mismatch repair

d) Nucleotide excision repair

61) DNA Helicase Enzyme Involved in Base Excision Repair Mechanism is

a) DNA helicase I

b) DNA helicase II

c) DNA helicase III

d) DNA helicase IV

62) Which of the Following Enzyme Involved in Base Excision Repair

a) DNA glycosylase

b) AP endonuclease

c) AP exonuclease

d) Both a and b

63) The Enzyme Photolyase Repairs the Thymine Dimer in the DNA by Which Mechanism?

a) Oxidation mechanism

b) Free radical mechanism

c) Direct bonding breaking

d) Adduct formation

64) The Gene which is Responsible for Human Breast Cancer?

a) BRCA 1

b) BRCA 2

c) BRCA 1 and 2

d) None of the above

65) Crossing over Links the two Pairs of Sister Chromatids Together at Points Called

a) Centrosome

b) Chiasmata

c) Bouquet

d) none

66) …….Small DNA Sequences That Move to Virtually any Position in a Cell's

a) Exons
b) Introns
c) LTRs
d) Transposons

67) The Point Mutation that Replaces a Purine with Another Purine or A Pyrimidine with Another Pyrimidine

a) Transition
b) Transversion
c) Nonsense
d) Missense mutation

68) The Process Involved in the RNA Formation on the DNA Template is

a) Translation
b) Transcription
c) Replication
d) Transformation

69) Transcription is the Transfer of Genetic Information from

a) DNA to protein
b) tRNA to mRNA
c) DNA to mRNA
d) mRNA to tRNA

70) Which Site of the tRNA Molecule Hydrogen Bonds to a mRNA Molecule?

a) Codons
b) Anticodons
c) 5' end of the tRNA
d) 3' end of the tRNA

71) Which One of the Enzymes that do Not Have Proofreading Activity?

a) DNA polymerase I

b) DNA polymerase II

c) DNA polymerase III

d) RNA Polymerase

72) RNA Polymerase in Prokaryotes has a Removable

a) Alpha subunit

b) Beta subunit

c) Both a and b

d) Sigma subunit

73) Transcription Begins at

a) At the start codon

b) Upstream from the start codon

c) Downstream from the start codon

d) None of these

74) In Prokaryotes, Transcription is

a) Terminated by the stop codon

b) Terminated by a protein called rho

c) Terminated by a poly a sequence

d) Terminated by a start codon

75) In Eukaryotes, the RNA Polymerase Responsible for Transcription of mRNA is

a) RNA polymerase I

b) RNA polymerase II

c) RNA polymerase III

d) None of the above

76) Rifampicin Inhibits Bacterial RNA Synthesis by Binding to the ....Subunit of RNA Polymerase

a) Alpha subunit

b) Beta subunit

c) Sigma subunit

d) Omega subunit

77) Which Single Nucleotide Makes up the 5' cap?

a) Guanine

b) Adenine

c) Cytosine

d) uracil

78) Modification of the 5'ends of Eukaryotic mRNA is called……

a) Capping

b) Polyadenylation

c) Splicing

d) Transcription

79) How many Residues are Present in Poly (A) Tail of Eukaryotic mRNA

a) 70- 150

b) 80-250

c) 40-60

d) 100-150

80) Which of the Following is not a Post-Transcriptional Modification?

a) Splicing

b) 5'capping

c) 3' polyadenylation

d) glycosylation

81) Real Time PCR is Useful for

a) Quantification of DNA

b) Amplification of DNA

c) Checking of expression profile

d) All of the above

Answer

1.a, 2.d, 3.a, 4.d, 5.c, 6.b, 7.b, 8.a, 9.d, 10.b, 11.a, 12.b, 13.b, 14.b, 15.a, 16.a, 17.d, 18.a, 19.d, 20.a, 21.d, 22.b, 23.a, 24.a, 25.a, 26.c, 27.c, 28.a, 29.b, 30.a, 31.d, 32.b, 33.c, 34.b, 35.d, 36.c, 37.c, 38.a, 39.a, 40.d, 41.b, 42.b, 43.a, 44.b, 45.a, 46.c, 47.b, 48.c, 49.a, 50.a, 51.c, 52.b, 53.b, 54.a, 55.a, 56.c, 57.b, 58.d, 59.d, 60.b, 61.d, 62.b, 63.b, 64.b, 65.d, 66.a, 67.b, 68.c, 69.b, 70.d, 71.d, 72.b, 73.b, 74.b, 75.b, 76.a, 77.a, 78.d, 79.d, 80.d.

Chapter - 3

Veterinary and Animal Husbandry Extension

Dr. Anupama Jena and Dr. Sadhna Ojha

1) The Word 'Extension' is Derived From........ Root.

a) Greek

b) Latin

c) French

d) Portuguese

2) Agricultural Extension is a .... Type of Education.

a) Formal

b) Informal

c) Non-formal

d) Technical

3) Who Categorized Education as Formal, Informal and Non-Formal?

a) Coombs and Ahmed

b) Leagan

c) Stewart

d) Dube

4) Successful Management of Resources to Satisfy Changing Human Needs, While Maintain and Enhancing Quality of Environment and Conservation of Natural Resources is called as......

a) Development

b) Conservation

c) Profitability

d) Sustainability

5) The use of the Term Extension Originated in England in…… Year.

a) 1866

b) 1873

c) 1876

d) 1878

6) Who first Conceptualized Extension as an Applied Science?

a) James Stewart

b) Paul Leagan

c) Ensminger

d) NCA

7) There are how many Levels of Extension?

a) 1

b) 2

c) 4

d) 5

8) Who said that Basic Philosophy of Extension Education is How to Think, not what to think?

a) Coombs and Ahmed

b) Leagan

c) Kelsey and Hearne

d) Morgan

9) Extension Education Process is developed by……

a) James Stewart

b) Paul Leagan

c) Ensminger

d) Dale

10) Extension Education Process consists of how many Steps?

a) 3

b) 7

c) 8

d) 5

11) **……is the Process through Which an Individual, through one's Own Efforts and Abilities Changes the Behaviour?**

a) Teaching

b) Process

c) Learning

d) None of the above

12) **Who Developed Cone of Experience?**

a) Coombs and Ahmed

b) Leagan

c) Dale

d) Morgan

13) **We tend to remember…… % of what we See and Hear?**

a) 30%

b) 50%

c) 70%

d) 90%

14) **We tend to remember…… % of what we Read?**

a) 10%

b) 30%

c) 70%

d) 90%

15) **…….is the Pursuit of Wisdom, a Body of General Principles or Laws of a Field of Knowledge.**

a) Philosophy

b) Principle

c) Objective

d) Knowledge

16) **A Generalized Guideline which Forms the Basis for Decision and Action in a Consistent way is……**

a) Philosophy

b) Principle

c) Objective

d) Knowledge

17) Which Principle Says "Change Should Start From the Existing Situation"

a) Principle of Cultural difference

b) Grass root principle

c) Interest and need principle

d) Principle of participation

18) …….is the Application of Knowledge for the Practical Purpose.

a) Practice

b) Learning

c) Technology

d) Adoption

19) Who Proposed Steps of Extension Teaching?

a) Dale

b) Morgan

c) Leagan

d) Wilson and Gallup

20) ……is an Inner State That Energizes, Activates or Moves and Directs Human Behaviour towards Goals.

a) Psychology

b) Motivation

c) Leadership

d) All of the above

21) In Urban Society….. is the Work Unit?

a) Individual

b) Group

c) Family

d) Non-of the above

22) Value System is Sacred in……

a) Rural society

b) Urban society

c) Mixed society

d) all of the above

23) …….is a Group Defined by Sex Relationship.

a) In-group
b) Out group
c) Family
d) Non-of the above

24) ……is a Society in Which Relationships are Traditional or Personal or often both.

a) Gemeinschaft
b) Gesellschaft
c) Community
d) Non-of the above

25) What is the Type of Family where the Determination of Descent and Property Inheritance Takes Place along the Male Line?

a) Patri-local
b) Patri-lineal
c) Patriarchal
d) None of the above

26) ……is The Type of Group with which Individuals can't Identify Themselves.

a) Voluntary group
b) Involuntary group
c) Informal group
d) Non-of the above

27) What is that type of Group called when the Individuals does not Have any Choice or is not required to Put any Effort?

a) Voluntary group
b) Involuntary group
c) Informal group
d) Non-of the above

28) Continuous Geographic area is a Feature of......

a) Society

b) Group

c) Community

d) All of the above

29) Achievement of Goal is Priority in........

a) Competition

b) Conflict

c) Cooperation

d) Assimilation

30) Making the Other Party Ineffectual is Main Feature of......

a) Competition

b) Conflict

c) Cooperation

d) Assimilation

31) ......is Belief in Supernatural.

a) Culture

b) Religion

c) Both of these

d) Non-of these

32) ......Denotes The Complex Whole Which Includes Knowledge, Belief, Art, Morals, Laws, Custom and Other Capabilities and Habits Acquired by People as Member of Society.

a) Culture

b) Religion

c) Belief

d) Non-of these

33) Mental Convictions one has About the Truth or Actuality of Something is......

a) Culture

b) Value

c) Belief

d) Non-of these

34) Which Among the Following is the Informal ways of Behaviour?

a) Folkways

b) Mores

c) Norms

d) Values

35) Socially Acceptable ways of Behaviour is……

a) Folkways

b) Mores

c) Norms

d) Values

36) Group Centered Leadership is………

a) Optimistic and positive

b) Pessimistic and negative

c) Optimistic and negative

d) Non-of the above

37) ……Involves Alternation in Structure and Function of Society.

a) Social stratification

b) Social in-equilibrium

c) Social change

d) all of the above

38) When the Rate of Change in a Social System is Commensurate with The System's Ability to Cope with it is called as……?

a) Stable equilibrium

b) Dynamic equilibrium

c) Disequilibrium

d) Non-of the above

39) Pre-Judgment Regarding Something is……

a) Prejudice

b) Stereotype

c) Both

d) None

40) ....Are Fixed Images Formed in One's Mind About People, Practices or Various Other Social Phenomena on The Basis of Experience, Attitude, Values, Impressions or Without any Direct Experience.

a) Prejudice

b) Stereotype

c) Both

d) None

41) Who gave the Idea of Conditional Learning?

a) Thorndike

b) Pavlov

c) Tolman

d) None

42) Innovation is Dependent on time

a) Yes

b) No

43) A Decision to make full use of Innovation as The Best Course of Action Available is......

a) Adoption

b) Diffusion

c) Innovation

d) Communication

44) The Process by Which an Innovation is communicated through Certain Channels over time among the Members of Social System is called as......

a) Adoption

b) Diffusion

c) Innovation

d) Communication

45) An Idea, Practice or Object that is observed as New by an individual or other unit of Adoption is……

a) Adoption
b) Diffusion
c) Innovation
d) Communication

46) Which among these is not a Perceived Attribute of Innovation?

a) Relative advantage
b) Compatibility
c) Complexity
d) Feasibility

47) Which Among These Attributes is Negatively Related to Innovation?

a) Relative advantage
b) Compatibility
c) Complexity
d) Trialability

48) The 6th Attribute of Innovation is………

a) Predictability
b) Feasibility
c) Adoptability
d) countable

49) ……is an Idea that an Individual Adopts at one Point in Time in Order to Lower the Probability that Some Future Unwanted Event will occur.

a) Relative advantage
b) Compatibility
c) Preventive innovation
d) None

50) Who First Recognized that Adoption of New Idea Consisted of Stages?

a) Ryan and Gross

b) Wilkening

c) Singh

d) None

51) According to Singh Adoption Process Consists of How Many Stages?

a) 4

b) 5

c) 7

d) 8

52) Who Said Stages of Adoption are Dynamic and Sometimes one Stage Appear more than once?

a) Ryan and Gross

b) Wilkening

c) Singh

d) None

53) Innovation-Decision Process Consists of how many Stages?

a) 4

b) 5

c) 7

d) 8

54) Which is the Correct Sequence of Innovation-Decision Process?

a) KDPIC

b) KPDIC

c) PKDIC

d) PKIDC

55) The more Persons Involved in Innovation Decision Process will...... The Rate of Adoption.

a) Slower

b) Accelerate

c) No effect

d) Cannot say

56) Reinvention Occurs at which Stage of Innovation Decision Process?

a) Knowledge
b) Persuasion
c) Decision
d) Implementation

57) In which Stage Individual tries to avoid Conflicting Messages?

a) Knowledge
b) Persuasion
c) Confirmation
d) Implementation

58) Who is more likely to discontinue an Innovation?

a) Early adopters
b) Late adopters
c) Both
d) None

59) Never really considering the use of Innovation?

a) Active rejection
b) Passive rejection
c) Both
d) None

60) Decision to Reject an Innovation as a Result of Dissatisfaction with its Performance is......

a) Disenchantment discontinuance
b) Replacement discontinuance
c) Both
a) None

61) Who among the Following have Shorter Innovation-Decision Period?

a) Earlier adopters
b) Later adopters
c) Both
d) None

62) Diffusion of Non-Profit Products and Services is called as……?

a) Mandate of adoption

b) Social marketing

c) Both

d) None

63) When System Exerts Pressure on The Individual to Recognize the Relative Advantage of an Innovation is called as……?

a) Over adoption

b) Mandate of adoption

c) Social marketing

d) ALL of the above

64) Which among the Following is the Result of Adopters' Inability to Perceive the Consequences or Status Conferring Nature?

a) Over adoption

b) Mandate of adoption

c) Social marketing

d) All of the above

65) Individual is Supreme in Decision Making?

a) Optional innovation decision

b) Collective innovation decision

c) Authority innovation decision

d) Non-of the above

66) Individual has no Authority in Decision Making?

a) Optional innovation decision

b) Collective innovation decision

c) Authority innovation decision

d) Non-of the above

67) Increase Pressure from Interpersonal Networks may be termed as…..

a) Adoption effect

b) Innovation effect

c) Diffusion effect

d) All of the above

68) Which Channel of Communication was more important at Persuasion Stage in Innovation-Decision Process?

a) Mass media

b) Interpersonal

c) Both

d) None

69) Cosmopolite Channels are more important at...... Stage?

a) Knowledge

b) Persuasion

c) Both

d) None

70) Adoption of Innovation Normally Follows...... Shaped Curve when Plotted over Time on Frequency Basis?

a) Bell shaped

b) S-shaped

c) Both

d) None

71) Cumulative Number of Adopters with Time Follows a.... Shaped Curve?

a) Bell shaped

b) S-shaped

c) Both

d) None

72) Drones are the...... Members

a) Most innovative

b) Least innovative

c) Both

d) None

73) Deliberate is the term used for which Category.......

a) Early adopters

b) Innovators

c) Early majorit

d) Laggards

74) Who are Cautious and Skeptical?

a) Early adopters
b) Innovators
c) Early majority
d) Late majority

75) Who Constitute one Third of Total Adopters?

a) Early adopters
b) Innovators
c) Early majority
d) Laggards

76) Which Category Falls under Mean Minus two Standard Deviations to Mean Minus one Standard Deviation?

a) Early adopters
b) Innovators
c) Early majority
d) Laggards

77) Innovators includes…….. Percentage of Individuals in the Society?

a) 16%
b) 13.5%
c) 34%
d) 2.5%

78) Laggards Constitute….. Percentage of Individuals in the Society

a) 16%
b) 13.5%
c) 34%
d) 2.5%

79) Who Developed Adoption Index?

a) Singh
b) Wilkenin
c) Dasgupta
d) Bose

80) What is that Point Called when Enough Individuals have Adopted an Innovation so that Innovations Further rate of Adoption Becomes Self-Sustaining?

a) Sustainability

b) Saturation

c) Fidelity

d) Critical mass

81) National Demonstration was launched in Which Year?

a) 1962

b) 1964

c) 1971

d) 1979

82) ORP Was Initiated in......?

a) 1964

b) 1971

c) 1974

d) 1979

83) The First KVK Was Established at......

a) Puducherry

b) Nilokheri

c) Anand

d) Jorhat

84) Which Programme was Launched on The Occasion of Icar's Golden Jubilee Celebration?

a) National demonstration

b) KVK

c) ORP

d) L to L

85) Technology Projects of The ICAR get Merged with KVK was Effective from……

a) 1990

b) 1992

c) 1995

d) 1998

86) EEI Jorhat Assam, was Started on……

a) 1959

b) 1962

c) 1979

d) 1987

87) Manage provides training to…….

a) Lower level extension professionals

b) Middle level extension professional

c) Upper level extension professionals

d) Non-of them

88) Each Project had an Operational area of about……… Square Miles in CDP?

a) 200-300

b) 400-500

c) 300-500

d) 500-700

89) Each Project in CDP Comprises…… no of Villages and…… Population?

a) 200, 20000

b) 300, 20000

c) 250, 2 lakhs

d) 300, 2 lakhs

90) and……… Population?

a) 100, 65 thousand

b) 150, 70 thousand

c) 100, 70 thousand

d) 150, 65 thousand

91) The Concept of Community Development has originated from……

a) Oxford

b) Sanford

c) Cambridge

d) None

92) The first State to Adopt Panchayati Raj?

a) Gujrat

b) Rajasthan

c) Maharashtra

d) Tamilnadu

93) The Phase of Stagnation of Panchayati Raj in India was……

a) 1959-64

b) 1965-69

c) 1969-77

d) None of these

94) 'Contact Farmer' Concept Came in India through which Programme?

a) KVK

b) NATP

c) IRDP

d) T & V

95) The Word Entrepreneur was Proposed By……

a) Marx

b) Cantillon

c) Drucker

d) Schumpter

96) Who called Entrepreneurs as Social Parasite?

a) Marx
b) Cantillon
c) Drucker
d) Schumpter

97) Sam Pitroda was…… Type Entrepreneur?

a) Mobile
b) Managerial
c) Empire builder
d) Innovative

98) Niesbud is present in……

a) Agra
b) Lucknow
c) New Delhi
d) Bhopal

99) Birla is…… Type Entrepreneur?

a) Mobile
b) Managerial
c) Empire builder
d) Innovative

100) Entrepreneurs are……

a) Low risk taker
b) Moderate risk taker
c) High risk taker
d) don't taker

101) World youth day is celebrated on……?

a) 6th June
b) 12th July
c) 21st March
d) 1st December

102) Who Proposed 4 Levels of Communication?

a) Leagan
b) Berlo
c) Hovland
d) Thayer

103) What is the most important Element in Communication?

a) Communicator
b) Receiver
c) Message
d) Channel

104) Communication Comes from a......... Term?

a) Greek
b) French
c) Arabic
d) Latin

105) According to Berlo the Purpose of Communication is......?

a) To influence
b) Immediate and delayed reward
c) Persuasion
d) Consumatory

106) Effectiveness of Communication does not depend on which among These Factors?

a) Comprehension
b) Validity
c) Utility
d) None of these

107) Which Communication Model has Some Political Influence?

a) Aristotle
b) Berlo
c) Lasswell
d) Schramm

108) Who Proposed Organic Nature of Communication?

a) Aristotle

b) Berlo

c) Lasswell

d) Schramm

109) Noise is an Important Element in Which Communication Model?

a) Berlo

b) Shannon-weaver

c) Schramm

d) Hovland

110) Who Proposed Linguistic Theory of Communication?

a) Berlo

b) Shannon-weaver

c) Williams

d) Leagans

111) Social Distance is……

a) 18 inch

b) 18inch-4 feet

c) 4-8 feet

d) More than 8 feet

112) Emphasizing Connotative Meaning Increases…… and Decreases……..

a) Fidelity, Readability

b) Readability, Fidelity

c) Can't say

d) None of the above

113) Which among the Following is a hot Medium?

a) Radio

b) Television

c) Telephone

d) None of the above

114) Which among these Skills Crucial to both Encoding and Decoding?

a) Writing

b) Speaking

c) Listening

d) Thought of reasoning

115) What is that Quality of Speaker that is Personally Appealing to the Listener?

a) Knowledge level

b) Extrovert

c) Skill

d) Ethos

116) Who Introduced the Concept of Communication Economy?

a) Berlo

b) Shannon-weaver

c) Thayer

d) Leagans

117) According to Berlo Message has the Following Components Except.

a) Code

b) Content

c) Treatment

d) Concept

118) Information Flows Direct the Masses Waiting to Receive it, with Nothing Intervening

a) Hypo-dermic needle model

b) Two-step flow model

c) One-step flow model

d) None of the above

119) Type of Distortion?

a) Fog distortion

b) Mirage distortion

c) Both

d) None of the above

120) Media Forum is a Combination of………

a) Mass media and interpersonal channel

b) Mass media and group channels

c) Both

d) None of the above

121) Minimum amount of Light is lost by Which Projection Method?

a) Direct projection

b) Indirect projection

c) Reflected projection

d) None of the above

122) Lantern Slide Projector is follows…… Projection System?

a) Direct projection

b) Indirect projection

c) Reflected projection

d) None of the above

123) Opaque Projector uses which Projection System?

a) Direct projection

b) Indirect projection

c) Reflected projection

d) None of the above

124) Projection beyond 25 Degree is used in which type of Screen?

a) Beaded Screen

b) Matte screen

c) Both of these

d) None of these

125) For Three Dimensional Objects which kind of Screen is used?

a) Beaded Screen

b) Matte screen

c) Silver screen

d) Lenticular screen

126) A Film Strip Normally Contains...... Number of Full Frames?

a) 20-36

b) 40-72

c) 35-70

d) None of the above

127) A Three Dimensional Imitation of a Thing in Certain aspects Only for the Purpose of Learning, So it may not be Similar in Appearance

a) Object

b) Model

c) Mock-ups

d) All of the above

128) According to Whom Audio-Visual Aids is an Instructional Device that can be Heard and Seen

a) Dale

b) Kinder

c) Ahluwalia

d) Haas and Packer

129) By Hearing..... Learning Takes Place?

a) 87%

b) 7%

c) 3.5%

d) 1.5%

130) Printed Books are...... Generation Media?

a) 1st

b) 2nd

c) 3rd

d) 4th

131) Television is...... Generation Media?

a) 1st
b) 2nd
c) 3rd
d) 4th

132) Dale Classified Extension Teaching Methods According to.......

a) Use
b) Form
c) Contribution to learning
d) None of the above

133) Peripatetic Team Meeting is......

a) Individual contact method
b) Group contact method
c) Mass contact method
d) None of the above

134) Agricultural Clinic is a....... Method?

a) Spoken
b) Visual
c) Spoken and visual
d) None of the above

135) ......is An Intensive Teaching Activity?

a) Exhibition
b) Campaign
c) Meeting
d) Method demonstration

136) Which Programme Was Proposed to Bridge the Gap Between Well-Developed Research Systems With That of Extension System?

a) NAEP
b) NREP
c) NARP
d) NAIP

137) District?

a) Thanjavur

b) Aligarh

c) Sahabad

d) Samastipur

138) SGRY Was Proposed by Merging Two Programs……?

a) NREP+ RLEGP

b) EAS+ SGRY

c) JRY + SGSY

d) None of the above

139) Under Bharat Nirman Programme Which among the Following Key Area was Not Identified for Improvement?

a) Primary education

b) Housing

c) Roads

d) Telephone

140) NDP-I was Launched on……

a) 2011

b) 2012

c) 2014

d) 2016

141) "Beti Bachao Beti Padhao" Yojana Was Launched on……

a) 22nd January, 2015

b) 14th Nov, 2014

c) 25th sep, 2014

d) 11 oct, 2014

142) To Encourage Multinational as well as National Companies to Manufacture Their Products in India which Programme was Launched?

a) Skill India

b) Start-up India

c) Make in India

d) None of the above

143) Rastriya Gokul Mission was Launched in......... Year?

a) 22nd January, 2015

b) 14th Nov, 2014

c) 16th Dec 2014

d) 11 oct, 2014

144) E-Pashuhaat Portal Launched by GOI is focused towards......

a) Marketing of animals

b) Health of animal

c) Availability of bovine germ plasm

d) None of the above

145) First Organic State......

a) Assam

b) Sikkim

c) Mizoram

d) Nagaland

146) Agricultural Education Day......

a) 25th November

b) 21st June

c) 24th April

d) 3rd December

147) In Farmer First, 'R' Stands For......

a) Result

b) Resources

c) Responsibility

d) Record

148) DD Kisan Launched on

a) 25th November, 2014

b) 26th May, 2015

c) 24th April, 2016

d) 3rd December, 2017

149) Toll Free Number of Kian Call Center……

a) 1800-180-1551

b) 1800-425-1551

c) 1800-180-1881

d) 1800-425-6761

150) ICAR was established on……

a) 1st April, 1920

b) 21st May 1890

c) 28th July 1932

d) 16th July, 1929

Answer

1.b, 2.c, 3.a, 4.d, 5.a, 6.b, 7.b, 8.c, 9.b, 10.d, 11.c, 12.c, 13.b, 14.a, 15.a, 16.b, 17.b, 18.c, 19.d, 20.b, 21.a, 22.a, 23.c, 24.a, 25.b, 26.c, 27.b, 28.c, 29.a, 30.b, 31.b, 32.a, 33.c, 34.a, 35.b, 36.a, 37.c, 38.b, 39.a, 40.b, 41.b, 42.b, 43.a, 44.b, 45.c, 46.d, 47.c, 48.a, 49.c, 50.a, 51.c, 52.c, 53.b, 54.b, 55.a, 56.d, 57.c, 58.b, 59.b, 60.a, 61.a, 62.b, 63.b, 64.a, 65.a, 66.c, 67.c, 68.b, 69.a, 70.a, 71.b, 72.b, 73.c, 74.d, 75.c, 76.a, 77.d, 78.a, 79.d, 80.d, 81.b, 82.c, 83.a, 84.d, 85.b, 86.d, 87.b, 88.b, 89.d, 90.a, 91.c, 92.b, 93.b, 94.d, 95.b, 96.a, 97.a, 98.c, 99.c, 100.b, 101.b, 102.d, 103.b, 104.d, 105.a, 106.d, 107.c, 108.d, 109.b, 110.c, 111.c, 112.b, 113.a, 114.d, 115.d, 116.c, 117.d, 118.a, 119.b, 120.a, 121.a, 122.b, 123.c, 124.b, 125.c, 126.a, 127.c, 128.d, 129.b, 130.b, 131.d, 132.c, 133.b, 134.a, 135.b, 136.a, 137.d, 138.b, 139.a, 140.b, 141.a, 142.c, 143.c, 144.c, 145.b, 146.d, 147.b, 148.b, 149.a, 150.d.

Chapter - 4

Animal Nutrition

Dr. Jatin Kumar Sahoo and Dr. Prasanta Kumar K Mishra

1) **Lactose Contains One Molecule of**
   a) Glucose and Glucose
   b) Glucose and Fructose
   c) Glucose and Galactose
   d) Fructose and Galactose
2) **In Birds Excess Nitrogen is Excreted as**
   a) Urea
   b) Uric acid
   c) Ammonia
   d) Nitrogen
3) **Fat Provides… Times more Energy than that of Carbohydrate and Protein**
   a) 2
   b) 2.5
   c) 1.5
   d) 2.25
4) **Fish oils are Rich in Which Fatty Acids**
   a) Linoleic acid
   b) Linolenic acid
   c) Arachidonic acid
   d) Levulenic acid
5) **Linkage present in Cellulose is**
   a) α (1-4)
   b) β (1-4)
   c) A (1-6)
   d) β (2-1)

6) Component of Hemicellulose Found in Silage is

a) Ribose
b) Arabinose
c) Both
d) None of the above

7) The Indigestible Fraction Present in Crude Fiber Includes

a) Cellulose
b) Hemicellulose
c) Lignin
d) All

8) Embden-Meyerhof-Parnas Pathway Occurs in which Part of the Cell

a) Cytoplasm
b) Golgibody
c) Mitochondria
d) Endoplasmic reticulum

9) The Synthesis of Glucose From the Non-Carbohydrate Molecules Such as Lactate is Called as

a) Glycolysis
b) Lactogenesis
c) Gluconeogenesis
d) None of the above

10) Disulphide Linkage Present in

a) Collagen
b) Keratin
c) β- Keratin
d) All of the above

11) Exudative Diathesis in Chicks is Caused By

a) Excess of vit C
b) Deficiency of Copper
c) Deficiency of Vit E
d) All

12) Which Water Solublevitamin Contain Straight Chain Instead of Ring Structure

a) Thiamine

b) Riboflavin

c) Cyanocobalamine

d) Pantothenic acid

13) Antimetabolite of Biotin is

a) Amprolium

b) Sulfonamide

c) Avidin

d) All

14) The Major end Product of Carbohydrate Digestion in Non Ruminant is

a) Glucose

b) Carbon dioxide

c) Volatile fatty acid

d) All of the above

15) The Major end Product of Carbohydrate Digestion in Ruminants is

a) Glucose

b) Methane

c) Volatile fatty acid

d) Water

16) The Energy Lost as Methane in Ruminants is.

a) 7- 13% of GE

b) 11% of DE

c) Both

d) No loss of energy

17) The Hormone Responsible for the Passage of Glucose from Blood into the Cell is

a) Glucagon

b) Insulin

c) Cortisol

d) Adrenaline

18) Vitamin Play Important role in Transamination of Amino acids is

a) B_{12}

b) B_3

c) B_6

d) B_5

19) Nitrogen Corrected ME Value Per Gram of Nitrogen for Ruminants is

a) 7.4 Kcal

b) 6.7 Kcal

c) 8.1 Kcal

d) 9.4 Kcal

20) The Hormone that Controls Blood Calcium is

a) Calcitonin

b) Thyroxine

c) Parathyroid hormone

d) Both a and c

21) Carbonic Anhydrase is a Metallo Enzyme Containing

a) Mn

b) Fe

c) Zn

d) Cu

22) Scaly Wool is Produced Due to Deficiency of

a) Cu

b) Zn

c) S

d) Mn

23) Most Limiting Amino Acid in Cereal Proteins is

a) Leucine

b) Methionine

c) Lysine

d) Cysteine

24) Salt is Added to the Diet as

a) 0.5% of ration DM

b) 1% of concentrate mixture

c) 3% of Concentrate mixture

d) Both a and b

25) One Gram Methane Contains...... Kilo Caloriesof Energy

a) 13.34

b) 2.53

c) 9.65

d) 11.4

26) 1 kg TDN is Equivalent to

a) 4.41 McalME

b) 3.616 Mcal DE

c) 0.869 Kg SE

d) All

27) The Toxic Principle Present in Jatropha is

a) Ricin

b) Mimosin

c) Phorbol ester

d) Cyanogen

28) Anti-Nutritional Factor Present in Mango Seed Kernel

a) Cyanogen

b) Saponin

c) Tannin

d) All the above

29) Crops Suitable for Ensiling Must be Rich in

a) Protein

b) Fat

c) Soluble sugars

d) All of the above

30) Mycotoxins Best Known For Showing Oestrogenic Syndrome in Swine is

a) Aflatoxins

b) Trichothecenes

c) Zearalenone

d) Fumonisins

31) Sway Back in Lambs is Due to Deficiency of

a) Mg

b) Se

c) Cu

d) Zn

32) Starch Equivalent Values are Developed by

a) Thomas and Mitchel

b) E.W. Crampton

c) Oscar Kellner

d) None of the above

33) Non-Ruminant Herbivore is

a) Rabbit

b) Deer

c) Elephant

d) Both a and c

34) To Minimize Sulphur Deficiency in Urea Feeding, 1 Gram Urea Should be Given Along with

a) 1 g sodium sulphate

b) 0.5 g anhydrous sodium sulphate

c) 0.13 g anhydrous sodium sulphate

d) 0.5 g sodium metabisulphite

35) Mineral Act as Coenzyme During Tryptophan to Niacin Conversion

a) Co

b) Zn

c) Fe

d) Mn

36) During Gross Energy Estimnation in Bomb Calorimeter Which Substance Taken as Standard

a) Formic acid

b) Benzoic acid

c) Citric acid

d) Oxalic acid

37) Urinary Energy Loss in Cattle is

a) 4-5% of GE

b) 2-3% of ME

c) Less during hay feeding than straw

d) All of above

38) First Respiration Calorimeter Constructed by Rubner for

a) Human

b) Guinea pig

c) Dog

d) Large animal

39) The Indian Scientist Remembered for The Developments of Methods to Estimate Minerals in Feeds and Fodders is

a) S.N. Ray

b) S.K. Ranjhan

c) S.K. Talapatra

d) N.d. Keher

40) The Scientist Introduced the Balance and Thermometer Into Nutrition Studies is

a) E.R. Orskov

b) W.N. Garret

c) Max Kleiber

d) Lavoisier

41) Scientist Discovered the Rumen Bacteria

a) R.E. Hungate

b) Gurby and Delafond

c) Henrik Dam

d) C.G. Orpin

42) Which of the Feeding Standards Provide Margin of Safety

a) NRC

b) ICAR

c) BIS

d) ARC

43) Legumes are Rich in

a) Calcium

b) Manganese

c) Phosphorus

d) Sodium

44) Out of Major Mineral, which Mineral Concentration in Body is Low

a) Calcium

b) Phosphorus

c) Potassium

d) Magnesium

45) Fat, The Most Variable Component of Body Relate to

a) Fat α 1/water

b) Fat α age

c) Fat α water

d) Both a and b

46) Moisture Concentration of Concentrates viz. Oil Cakes is

a) 25%

b) 70%

c) 10%

d) 40%

47) Out of Six Proximate Principles, Which is Calculated by Difference Rather than Being Actually Analysed

a) Ether extract (EE)

b) Crude protein (CP)

c) Nitrogen free extract (NFE)

d) Total Ash (TA)

48) Which is not a True Carbohydrate

a) Hemicellulose
b) Inulin
c) Cellulose
d) Lignin

49) Which is Neutral Detergent Soluble

a) Hemicelluloses
b) Cellulose
c) Pectin
d) Lignin

50) Xylose is

a) Monosaccharide
b) Disaccharide
c) Trisaccharide
d) Not carbohydrate

51) The Linkage Present in Inulin

a) Glucose β (1-4)
b) Glucose α (1-4)
c) Glucose β (2-1)
d) Glucose α (2-1)

52) Which Amino Acid is Neutral

a) Methionine
b) Lysine
c) Leucine
d) Arginine

53) Imidazole Group Present in which Amino Acid

a) Tryptophan
b) Proline
c) Tyrosine
d) Histidine

54) In Acidic pH, the Amino Acid Behaviour is

a) Anion
b) Cation
c) Neutral
d) None of the above

55) Who Classified Amino Acid as Essential And Non-Essential Type

a) B.L. Oser
b) W.C. Rose
c) R.T. Holman
d) None of the above

56) Number of Essential Amino Acids for Ruminants

a) 10
b) 11
c) 8
d) None of the above

57) In Chicken which Amino Acid Required for Uric Acid Synthesis

a) Tryptophan
b) Arginine
c) Glycine
d) Methionine

58) Which Amino Acid is Used to Synthesize Niacin

a) Tyrosine
b) Methyl alanine
c) Phenyl alanine
d) Tryptophan

59) Molecular Weight (Length of Chain) of The Fatty Acid in Fat is Measured by

a) Acid value
b) Iodine value
c) Saponification value
d) Richert-Michell value

60) Rancidity of Oil Leads to Increase in

a) Iodine value
b) Acid value
c) Saponification number
d) All of the above

61) The Omega System of Classification of Fatty Acid was Given by

a) W.C. Rose
b) R.T. Holman
c) Max Rubner
d) K.C. Sen

62) Vegetable Oil are Excellent Sources of

a) Arachidonic acid
b) Linoleic acid
c) Linolenic acid
d) All of the above

63) More water is Conserved by which Type of Feed Consumption to Generate Metabolic Water

a) Protein
b) Carbohydrate
c) Fat
d) All of the above

64) Tolerance Level of Salt Consumption

a) Sheep> cattle> pig
b) Cattle > Sheep > pig
c) Pig > Sheep>cattle
d) Sheep> pig >cattle

65) Prehensile Organ for Horse is

a) Tongue
b) Lip
c) Pointed lower lip
d) None of the above

66) Pig Saliva Contain which Enzyme

a) α-amylase

b) β-amylase

c) Both

d) None of the above

67) Protease activity in Rumen is Highest for

a) Bacteria

b) Fungi

c) Protozoa

d) All of the above

68) Who is Post-Gastric Fermentator (s)

a) Swine

b) Horse

c) Rabbit

d) All of these

69) Optimum Rumen Temperature is

a) 30-35°C

b) 35-45°C

c) 38-40°C

d) Above 50°C

70) Feed supplies Both Bypass Protein and Bypass Fat is

a) Soyabean meal

b) Cotton seed meal

c) Groundnut meal

d) All of these

71) In birds which form of Carbohydrate is Fastest

a) Galactose

b) Glucose

c) Fructose

d) Mannose

72) Hexose Monophosphate Shunt or Pentose Cycle is

a) Used for production of NADPH and NADP

b) Alternation of glucose oxidation pathway

c) Required for synthesis of Ribose-5-P

d) All of these

73) Glycogen Content is Highest in Which Species

a) Cow

b) Goat

c) Horse

d) Birds

74) Formation of Body Fat from Carbohydrate was First Food was First Demonstrated by

a) Mc Collum and Davis

b) Mattil and Bishop

c) J.B. Lawis and J. H. Gilbert

d) D.B. Lorens and M. Maxwell

75) Urea Cycle Occurs in

a) Muscle

b) Liver

c) Kidney

d) All of these

76) 1 Mole of Methane Produce

a) 2 ATP

b) 1 ATP

c) 3 ATP

d) 4 ATP

77) Lactate and Acrylate Pathway of Carbohydrate Digestion Become Important in Ruminants During

a) Grain feeding

b) Roughage feeding

c) During sulphur deficiency

d) Both a & c

78) Major Gas Production in Rumen

a) Methane

b) Hydrogen

c) Carbon dioxide

d) Oxygen

79) In Acidic Condition Which Fatty Acid Absorb Faster

a) Acetic acid

b) Propionic acid

c) Butyric acid

d) Isovaleric acid

80) In Case of CHO Engorgement in Cattle it Reveals

a) Presence of gram positive bacteria

b) Presence of gram negative bacteria

c) Presence of protozoa

d) All of the above

81) Role of Gluconeogenesis and Lipogenesis is High in

a) Non-ruminant

b) Ruminant

c) Both

d) Pseudoruminant

82) Amino Acids Absorbed as

a) Triprptide> Dipeptide> Free amino acids

b) Neutral amino acids> Basic amino acids

c) L-forms> D-forms of amino acids

d) All of these

83) The Ideal Proportion of Degradable Protein and Bypass Protein is

a) 40% degradable, 60% bypass

b) 60% degradable, 40% bypass

c) 70% degradable, 30% bypass

d) 80% degradable, 20% bypass

84) Most Limiting Amino Acids in Microbial Protein is

a) Lysine and Methionine

b) Lysine and Tryptophan

c) Methionine and Threonine

d) All of the above

85) ATP Consumed for Production of 1 Mole of Urea is

a) 3 ATP

b) 4 ATP

c) 5 ATP

d) 6 ATP

86) Uric Acid Produced from which Nitrogenous Compound

a) Purine

b) Pyrimidine

c) Both

d) Urea

87) End Product of Purine Metabolism in Dalmatian Breed of Dog

a) Allantoin

b) Uric acid

c) Urea

d) All of these

88) Only Ketogenic Amino Acid is

a) Lysine

b) Leucine

c) Isoleucine

d) All of thee

89) Significant Property of Urea is

a) Deficient in sulphur containing amino acid

b) No energy value of its own

c) Deficient in all minerals

d) All of the above

90) Urea is Poorly Utilised

a) When concentrate mixture contains more than 18% CP

b) Complete diet containing more than 13% CP

c) Presence of highly soluble and easily digestible protein in diet

d) All of the above

91) Urea can be Successfully Incorporated

a) 2-3% of concentrate mixture

b) 15% of total dry matter of feed

c) 1% of total diet

d) Both a & b

92) Molasses are Excellent Source of Minerals Except

a) Calcium

b) Phosphorus

c) Magnesium

d) Sodium

93) The Recommended Level of Urea Treatment for Enrichment of Straw

a) 1-1.5%

b) 2-3%

c) 4-5%

d) 5-10%

94) Principal Site of Lipid Digestion is

a) Mouth

b) Stomach

c) Small intestine

d) Large intestine

95) Excretion Route of Cholesterol is

a) Urine

b) Faeces

c) Sweat

d) None of the above

96) Fat Absorption is Highest for

a) Longer chain of fatty acid
b) Shorter chain of fatty acid
c) Not dependent on chain length
d) None of the above

97) Metabolic Faecal Nitrogen is Related to

a) Body weight
b) Age of the animal
c) Feed intake
d) All of the above

98) Sugar that promotes calcium absorption

a) Glucose
b) Sacharose
c) Lactose
d) Fructose

99) Cannibalism in Chicks Seen Due to

a) Na deficiency
b) Salt deficiency
c) Decreased fibre in diet
d) All of the above

100) Mineral Helps in Propionate Metabolism is

a) Cu
b) Mn
c) Co
d) Se

101) Iodine Content of Thyroid Gland on DMB is

a) 1%
b) 0.1%
c) 0.01%
d) 0.001%

102) Higher Manganese Level May Interfere with Which Mineral Absorption

a) Cu

b) Co

c) Zn

d) Fe

103) Element Derived from Metabolic Process of Kidney is

a) Mn

b) Zn

c) Co

d) Fe

104) Knocked Knee Syndrome is Due to Toxicity of Mineral

a) Calcium

b) Magnesium

c) Fluorine

d) Selenium

105) Selenium Content in the Plant

a) Increase with maturity

b) Decrease with maturity

c) Not present

d) Seasonal dependent

106) Mineral Essential for Urease Activity of Rumen Microbes is

a) Chromium

b) Lithium

c) Nickel

d) Vanadium

107) Amino Acids Effective for Chelation that is Useful in Transport and Storage of Metal Ions

a) Cysteine

b) Methionine

c) Histidine

d) Both a and c

108) Number of β Ionine Ring Present in Carotene

a) 1

b) 2

c) 3

d) 4

109) Requirement of Which Vitamin is Decreased as The Level of Fat in The Diet is Increased

a) A

b) E

c) B_1

d) B_2

110) B-Complex Vitamin Having Potential Glucogenic and Antilipolytic Activity

a) Thiamin

b) Niacin

c) Folic acid

d) Ascorbic acid

111) Vitamin Absorbed as Intact Form in The Gut is

a) Riboflavin

b) Biotin

c) Pantothenic acid

d) All of the above

112) Vitamin Having no Antioxidant Activity

a) Vit E

b) Vit C

c) Vit B_1

d) All of the above

113) Which is not an Anabolic Hormone

a) Androgens

b) Oestrogens

c) Thyroxine

d) Somatotropin

114) Non Starch Polysaccharide Present in Barley or Rye Which Cause Sticky Droppings in Chicks

a) Arabinoxylans
b) B-glucans
c) Pectin lyase
d) All of the above

115) Examples of Prebiotics

a) Inulin
b) Oligofructose
c) Mannose oligosaccharides
d) All of the above

116) Which is not a Rabi Fodder

a) Bajra
b) Oats
c) Berseem
d) None of the above

117) Gelatinization of Starch Occurs in

a) Pelleting
b) Exploding
c) Steam rolling
d) All of the above

118) As Per BIS the Maximum Fat in Rat Feed is

a) 1%
b) 3%
c) 5%
d) 7%

119) Panther may be Provided with Beef at the Rate of

a) 3kg/day
b) 5kg/day
c) 7kg/day
d) 10 kg/day

120) Abomasal Displacement Caused by Feeding

a) High roughages

b) High concentrates

c) Low concentrates

d) Low roughages

121) Vivar Technique Comes Under

a) Semi *in vivo*

b) *In vitro*

c) *In vivo*

d) All

122) Feeding Standard that was Based on Digestible Nutrients Like Protein, Fat and Carbohydrate

a) Wolff's satandard

b) Grouven

c) Hay equivalent

d) Scaninavian feeding standard

123) Protein Requirement of Ruminant can be Best Given by Term

a) CP

b) DCP

c) MP

d) Both a and b

124) Minimum Fat % in Sheep Ration is Essential

a) a.3%

b) 4%

c) 5%

d) Dietary not essential

125) As Per BIS, 2007 Minimum Crude Protein % Should be Present in Pre Starter Feed is

a) 20

b) 22

c) 23

d) 24

126) The Percentage of Maintenance Requirements of Pigs can be Met Through VFA is

a) 20%
b) 30%
c) 40%
d) 55%

127) Cereal Grains that is Normally not used in Horse Diet

a) Oats
b) Barley
c) Maize
d) Wheat

128) Dog Food Usually Designated as Dinners

a) Dry dog foods
b) Semimoist dog foods
c) Canned dog foods
d) Dog biscuits

129) Cats are Unable to Synthesize Arachidonic Acid From Linoleic Acid Due to Lack of Enzyme

a) Delta 6 desaturase
b) Picolinic carboxylase
c) Desaturase
d) Hydroxydesaturase

130) Which is not True about Rabbit Nutrition

a) Hard pellet contain Lignocellulose
b) Colon content expelled as soft faeces
c) Coprophagy practised during night time in domestic rabbit
d) All

Answers

1.C, 2.B, 3.D, 4.B, 5.B, 6.B, 7.C, 8.A, 9.C, 10.B, 11.C, 12.D, 13.C, 14. A, 15.C, 16.C, 17.B, 18.C, 19.A, 20.D, 21.C, 22.A, 23.C, 24.D, 25.A, 26.C, 27.C, 28.C, 29.C, 30.C, 31.C, 32.C, 33.D, 34.C, 35.C, 36.B, 37.A, 38.C, 39.C, 40.D, 41.A, 42.C, 43.A, 44.D, 45.D, 46.C, 47.C, 48.D, 49.C, 50.A, 51.C, 52.C, 53.D, 54.B, 55.B, 56.D, 57.C, 58.D, 59.C, 60.B, 61.B, 62.C, 63.B, 64.A, 65.B, 66.A, 67.C, 68.D, 69.C, 70.B, 71.B, 72.D, 73.C, 74.C, 75.B, 76.B, 77.D, 78.C, 79.C, 80.D, 81.C, 82.D, 83.B, 84.A, 85.B, 86.A, 87.B, 88.B, 89.D, 90.D, 91.D, 92.B, 93.B, 94.C, 95.B, 96.B, 97.C, 98.C, 99.D, 100.C, 101.B, 102.D, 103.B, 104.C, 105.B, 106.C, 107.D, 108.B, 109.C, 110.B, 111.C, 112.C, 113.B, 114.B, 115.D, 116.A, 117.A, 118.C, 119.A, 120.B, 121.B, 122.A, 123.C, 124.A, 125.C, 126.B, 127.D, 128.C, 129.A, 130.B.

Chapter - 5

Livestock Products Technology

Dr. Sadhna Ojha and Dr. Anupama Jena

1) **Abattoir Term is Derived from French Word a batter which Means……..**
   a) Killing of animal
   b) Strike down
   c) Death of animal
   d) Fall down
2) **When Animal is slaughtered in Open Air, This Kind of Slaughter House is called……**
   a) Gambler
   b) Shamble
   c) Abattoir
   d) None of the above
3) **Principle Component of Meat is……**
   a) Skeletal muscle
   b) Smooth muscle
   c) Adipose tissue
   d) All of the above
4) **Skeletal Muscles are……. in Nature.**
   a) Striated and voluntary
   b) Striated and non-voluntary
   c) Smooth and non-voluntary
   d) None of the above

5) **Structural Unit of Muscle is.....**

a) Sarcomere

b) Sarcoplasm

c) Muscle fibre

d) T-tubule

6) **Thick and Thin Filaments are Made Up of...... Respectively.**

a) Myosin and actin

b) Myosin and tropomyosin

c) Actin and troponin

d) Titin and nebulin

7) **Functional Unit of Muscle is......**

a) Myofibre

b) Sarcomere

c) Myofibril

d) Z-line

8) **Lysozomes Contain Group of Proteolytic Enzymes Known as........**

a) Cathepsins

b) Catalase

c) Protease

d) Hydrolases

9) **In Cardiac Muscles, the Contractile Layer is....**

a) Endocardium

b) Pericardiu

c) Myocardoium

d) Epicardium

10) **Connective Tissue Surrounding Muscle, Muscle Bundle and Muscle Fibre is Known As......**

a) Ground tissue

b) Extracellular fibres

c) Connective tissue proper

d) Mucoprotein

11) Connective Tissue Surrounding Muscle, Muscle Bundle and Muscle Fibre is Known as....

a) Ground tissue

b) Extracellular fibres

c) Connective tissue proper

d) Mucoprotein

12) Most Abundant Protein in Animal Body is....

a) Collagen

b) Elastin

c) Keratin

d) Reticulin

13) The Size of Muscle Fiber Bundle and Thickness of Ct Septa Determine...... of Meat.

a) Tenderness

b) Flavour

c) Texture

d) Juiciness

14) Intramuscular Fat is called as....

a) Marbling

b) Seam fat

c) Technical fat

d) All of the above

15) By Products Industry Contributes..... % of Total Income of Slaughter House.

a) 15-20

b) 20-25

c) 7-11

d) 2-4

16) The ATP Splitting Activity of Myosin ATPase is enhanced by... Ions.

a) Ca

b) Cl

c) Na

d) Mg

17) Is Calcium Sensitive Protein.

a) Troponin
b) Nebulin
c) Myosin
d) Titin

18) The Ultimate pH of Mammalian Muscle after Rigor Mortis is....

a) 6.2-6.4
b) 4.5-5.3
c) 5.4-5.6
d) 6.0-6.2

19) The Method for Making Meat Tenderer....

a) Electrical stimulation
b) Aging
c) Both A and B
d) All of the above

20) What is the Saturation Which Describes the Intensity of The Fundamental Color with respect to Amount of White Light that is mixed in with it.

a) Hue
b) Value
c) Chroma
d) None of the above

21) Chemical State of Iron in Oxymyoglobin and Metmyoglobin are...

a) +2, +3
b) +2, +2
c) +3, +2
d) +3, +3

22) ...is Taken as Part of Daily Food and Functions beyond Normal Limit.

a) Functional food
b) Designer food
c) Neutraceutical
d) None of the above

23) Number of Animals to be slaughtered per Hour or Per Day is known as....

a) Through put

b) Livestock unit

c) Out put

d) All of the above

24) A Small Abattoir has......

a) 1-2 acre land and upto 30,000 LU

b) 2-4 acre land and upto 50,000 LU

c) 4-6 acre land and >1 lakh LU

d) All of the above

25) Among the Following which Place is considered to be better for Abattoir Construction?

a) Rural site

b) Nominated industrial site

c) Urban site any of the above

26) One Drain is required for every....... Square Meters area in Slaughter House.

a) 35

b) 40

c) 45

d) 30

27) In Lairage....... Should be Given the Prime Importance.

a) Animal behaviour

b) Meat quality

c) Economics of abattoir

d) All of the above

28) In Canpak System, the Through Put is........ Animals/Hour.

a) 40-120

b) 185-190

c) 50-150

d) 130-180

29) The Storage Life of Beef at -18^{0}C is....... Months.

a) 9-12

b) 2-6

c) 8-24

d) 17-19

30) In Blood Meal, Protein Content is around...... %.

a) 80

b) 40

c) 60

d) 70

31) The Storage Life of Chicken under Refrigeration is....... Days.

a) 3-7

b) 14-18

c) 12-15

d) 1-3

32) In Halal Method of Slaughter, The Condemned Meat is called as.....

a) Halal

b) Haram

c) Shochit

d) Both A and B

33) Best Method for Preservation of Glands for Pharmaceuticals use is...... to Retards Autolysis and Bacterial Load.

a) Chilling

b) Pasteurization

c) Quick freezing

d) Sterilization

34) For Preparation of Rennin Following Micro Organisms are used.

a) Mucor pucillus

b) Methina coagulans

c) Both of the above

d) None

35) Slunk is the Hide Obtained From.....

a) Unborn calf

b) Steer

c) Mature heifer

d) Dead calf

36) In Dry Rendering, The Condition for Drying is.....

a) 75 psi for 3-5 hr

b) 40 psi for 8 hr

c) 40 psi for 3-5 hr

d) 75 psi for 7 hr

37) In Pithing, The Length of Rod Should not be More Than...

a) 0.6m

b) 0.5m

c) 0.7m

d) 0.3m

38) If Stunning to Sticking Interval if Higher, Chances of......... is high.

a) Slaughter spleen

b) Blood splashing

c) Electric shock

d) Missed shock

39) For Gas Stunning of Pigs, the Prescribed Percentage of CO_2 is....

a) 70-85%

b) 40-55%

c) 85-90%

d) 30-45%

40) In Jewish Method of Slaughter, The Removal of Blood Vessels is Known as.....

a) Kosher

b) Terefa

c) Porging

d) Al dabh

41) Following Diseases are usually Diagnosed during AM Examination.

a) Gid
b) Rabies
c) Lead poisoning
d) All of the above

42) No Carcass Splitting and no Brisket Opening are done in……

a) Buffalo
b) Sheep/goat
c) Horse
d) Pig

43) The Temperature of Sensory Room Should be…… °C.

a) 20-22
b) 25-27
c) 17-19
d) 30-35

44) The Amount of Sample Should be at Least….. Bites in Case of Solids and…… ml in Case of Liquids.

a) 2, 50
b) 2, 15
c) 5, 15
d) 5, 30

45) For Sensory Evaluation, There Should be not More than………. Sessions per Week.

a) 15
b) 10
c) 12
d) 5

46) The Temperature of Comminuted Meat Products for Sensory Evaluation Should be……. °C.

a) 35-40
b) 70
c) 50-60
d) 80

47) The Best Time for Sensory Evaluation is.....

a) Late morning
b) Late night
c) Late evening
d) Early morning

48) Odor is sensed at... Which Lies at the Top of the inside of The Nose.

a) Incus
b) Mallus
c) Stapes
d) Regio olfactoria

49) Reheating of Stored Cooked Meat Products Develop...... Flavor.

a) Oxidative flavor
b) Warmed over
c) Staled flavor
d) None of the above

50) In Flavor Profile testing...... Numbers of Trained Panelists are used.

a) 6-8
b) 4-5
c) 8-10
d) 3-4

51) Out of 19% of Protein Present in Muscle Tissue, Myofibrillar Protein is..... %

a) 6.5
b) 11.5
c) 14.5
d) 15.5

52) In Case of Canning, the Shelf Life of Meat in Retort Pouches is.... years.

a) 2
b) 1
c) Infinite
d) None

53) The Process of Subdivision or Reduction of Raw Meat into Meat Pieces or Particles in……

a) Preblending

b) Communition

c) Tumblin

d) All of the above

54) Meat Emulsion is……

a) Water in oil

b) Oil in water

c) Fat in water

d) None

55) Which of The Following is/are Emulsion Type Sausages?

a) Frankfurter

b) Salami

c) Thuringer

d) None

56) The Critical Control Points which can be Eliminated Completely are…..

a) CCP type 1

b) CCP type 2

c) Both A and B

d) None of the above

57) The…… Schedule of MFPO Deals with the Requirements to be complied with as Regards to Packaging, Marking and Labeling the Containers.

a) First

b) Second

c) Third

d) Fourth

58) Category…. Slaughter Houses under MFPO are Manufactures of Meat Products who Purchase Meat from Approved Slaughter Houses.

a) C

b) B

c) A

d) D

59) Prevention of Food Adulteration act was enacted in…..

a) 1973

b) 1951

c) 1955

d) 1957

60) Eighteen Pairs of Ribs are Found in…….. Which can be used to identify the Adulteration of Meat.

a) Pig

b) Horse

c) Dog

d) Buffalo

61) …..Meat is Richer in Glycogen as Compared to Other Food Animals.

a) Pig

b) Cattle

c) Sheep

d) Horse

62) Iodine Value of Lard is…..

a) 50-70

b) 71-86

c) 37-40

d) 36-46

63) The Amount of Thiamine is Higher in…as Compared to other Species.

a) Mutton

b) Pork

c) Carabeef

d) Chevon

64) ….is used to Retain Curing Solution in Product during Curing.

a) Ascorbate

b) Phosphate

c) BHT

d) Nitrate

65) The Inner Thick Layer of Albumin is also called as……

a) Latebra

b) Chalaziferous layer

c) Vitelline membrane

d) Germinal disc

66) Type 2 Black Rot in Egg is caused by…..

a) Proteus

b) Pseudomonas

c) Both A and B

d) None of the above

67) Type 1 Black Rot in Egg Gives…… Odor.

a) Faecal

b) Cabbage

c) Fishy

d) Hay like

68) Thermostablization Causes…… in Eggs.

a) Sealing of pores

b) Coagulation of protein

c) Thinning of shell

d) None of the above

69) India Stands….. In Goat and….. In Sheep Production.

a) First, sixth

b) Sixth, first

c) Second, fourth

d) Second, sixth

70) **Authorities called as...**

a) Halal

b) Schochit

c) Muftis

d) None of the above

71) **Lymph Nodes Draining to Muscle and Are of Special Interest of Meat Inspection are called as.....**

a) Meat lymph nodes

b) Red lymph nodes

c) Green lymph nodes

d) All of the above

72) **If Hide is branded on the but or on the side, it is called as......**

a) Colorado/texas hide

b) Country or small packer

c) Native hide

d) Renderer/murrain

73) **.....is a Term used for Leather with Wool Still Attached?**

a) Slat

b) Shearling

c) Murrain

d) Slunk skin

74) **The Equipment......... is used to Measure the Total Area of Leather, whose Fingers Sense the Leather when It Passes through the Machine.**

a) Planimeter

b) Texture analyzer

c) Sonicator

d) All of the above

75) **The Enzyme... Extracted from Testes is used as Spreading Factor.**

a) Hyaluronidase

b) Catalase

c) Oxidase

d) Reductase

76) Calves Slaughtered within Few Days of Birth Having Low Muscle: Bone Ratio and Very Edematous Carcass are called as……

a) Bobby calves

b) Fat stock

c) Lean calves

d) Still birth

77) Horse Meat is also called as….

a) Chevalin

b) Venison

c) Carabeef

d) None of the above

78) The Space between Outer Shell Membrane and Inner Shell Membrane in Egg is called as….

a) Air sac

b) Air space

c) Air cell

d) Latebra

79) Rabbit Meat is called as……

a) Levarette

b) Chevalli

c) Venison

d) None of the above

80) The Refractive Index of Horse Meat is Upto….

a) 61.5

b) 71.6

c) 53.5

d) 30

81) The Intensity of Light is usually……. Lux at Meat Inspection area.

a) 110

b) 540

c) 220

d) 650

82) The Recommended Water Requirement......... liters/pig, which is...... Than other Animals.

a) 454, higher

b) 54, higher

c) 454, lower

d) 90, higher

83) The Main Considerations of a Slaughter House are Dependent upon.....

a) Meat quality

b) Economics

c) Animal welfare

d) All of the above

84) The Temperature of Cutting Room/Processing Room Should be.....

a) 10-12

b) 15-17

c) 20-22

d) <7

85) Meat Must Be Immediately Chilled After Post Mortem at Not More than......

a) 7^0C

b) 10^0C

c) 11^0C

d) 5^0C

86) Father of Canning.......

a) Nicholas apart

b) Von ostertag

c) Hippocrats

d) None of the above

87) The Process of Separation of Intestine from Mesentry is called......

a) Running

b) Stripping

c) Bunging

d) Rodding

88) .....is a Measure of Oxygen Required for the Oxidation of all Organic Matter in a known Volume of Effluent using a Standard Technique?

a) COD

b) BOD

c) Oxidation value

d) None of the above

89) In Neck Stab or Evernazione Method of Slaughter, a Sharp Edged Knife is plunged into Occipito-Atlantal Space. The Knife is called as.....

a) Pith

b) Puntilla

c) Chocker

d) None of the above

90) In Canning Industry, The Indicator Organisms used for Commercial Sterility is.....

a) *Clostridium Botulinum*

b) *Staphylococcus aureus*

c) *E.*

d) *coli*

e) *Both A and B*

91) Black Spot in Meat is caused by.....

a) *Cladosporium herbarum*

b) *Sporotrichum carnis*

c) *Thaminidium*

d) *Both A and C*

92) White Spot is caused by....

a) *Cladosporium herbarum*

b) *Sporotrichum carnis*

c) *Thaminidium*

d) *Both A and B*

93) into Normal Position, Whereupon the Opposite end Bulges.

a) Flipper

b) Springer

c) Nitrate swell

d) Soft swell

94) Sulphur Stinker in Cans is caused by....

a) *Clostridium Botulinum*

b) *Cl. Nigrificans*

c) *Cl. Perfringenes*

d) *Cl. Coagulans*

95) A...... is a can with a Hole through which Air or Infection may Enter or its Contents Escape.

a) Leaker

b) Blower

c) Overfilled can

d) Black cap

96) In Homogenized Milk, the Sizes of Fat Globules are Less than......

a) 2 μ

b) 10μ

c) 20μ

d) 50μ

97) Normal pH of Milk is.......

a) 6.5-6.8

b) 7.3-7.5

c) 5.7-5.8

d) 4.5-4.6

98) Normal Acidity of Milk is Due to......

a) Phosphates

b) Citrates

c) Casein

d) All of the above

99) Normal specific gravity of milk is…..

a) 1.028-1.032

b) 1.034-1.036

c) 1.012-1.026

d) None of the above

100) For Testing of Platform Microbiology of Milk…….. Tests are done.

a) MBRT

b) Resazurin test

c) Only a

d) a and b

101) Double Tonned Milk Has….. % Fat and …. % SNF.

a) 1.5, 9.0

b) 4.5, 8.5

c) 3.0, 8.5

d) 2.0, 9.0

102) Dried Milk Powder is Made Instantly Soluble by Addition of Steam or Hot Water, This Process is called as……

a) Rehydration

b) Instantization

c) Hydration

d) None of the above

103) Homogenization of Milk is Done Mainly for……

a) To prevent separation of fat

b) To keep fat in emulsified form

c) To make milk more digestible

d) All of the above

104) During Preparation of Condensed Milk, Forced Crystallization is done by…..

a) Powdered refined lactose

b) Hydrated casein

c) Homogenized fat

d) All of the above

105) Mold Button in Condensed Milk is caused by……

a) Contamination of A. ripens

b) High temperature storage

c) Presence of oxygen

d) All of the above

106) Cheddaring is done for…….

a) Removal of moisture

b) For improving body and texture

c) Acidity upto 0.3%

d) All of the above

107) Cottage Cheese is prepared from……

a) Skimmed milk

b) Tonned milk

c) Recombined milk

d) Double tonned milk

108) Cottage Cheese is…….

a) Soft and UN ripened

b) Hard and ripened

c) Soft and unripened

d) Hard and unripened

109) Eye Formation and Nutty Flavor is Found in…….

a) Swiss cheese

b) Cheddar cheese

c) Camembert cheese

d) Roquefort cheese

110) Roquefort Cheese is Soft Cheese Having Sharp Flavor as fat is converted into….

a) FFA and ketones

b) Amides and ketones

c) Acids and amides

d) None of the above

111) Camembert Cheese is White Colored Cheese, Where Mold used is.....

a) Penicillium camemberti
b) Penicillium roqueforti
c) Bravibacterium linens
d) None of the above

112) Yoghurt is having....... Acidity than Curd.

a) Higher
b) Lower
c) Equal
d) Any of the above

113) Main flavoring compound in butter is....

a) Diacetyl
b) Propionic acid
c) Lactic acid
d) Alcohol

114) ......is Weight of Butter obtained from a Given Lot of Cream that Exceeds Amount of Fat Present in Cream.

a) Moisture content
b) Over run
c) Shrinkage
d) Both b and c

115) As Per PFA 1976, Total Solids Present in Ice Cream is not Less than.... %.

a) 26
b) 36
c) 40
d) 50

116) Emulsifier used in Ice Cream is for.....

a) Improve whipping quality
b) Smoothen body
c) Provide texture
d) All of the above

117) Over Run in Ice Cream is Due to.....

a) Incorporation of air

b) Moisture content

c) Solid content

d) Any of the above

118) In Milk, Major Amount of Protein is Casein that Process Around.... %

a) 80

b) 65

c) 55

d) 70

119) When Milk Stones React with Calcium Ions of Hard Water, They Form Harder Layers, Called as....

a) Hardening

b) Scaling

c) Stonning

d) None of the above

120) The Clarified Butter fat Product is......

a) Ghee

b) Curd

c) Cheese

d) None of the above

121) As Per PFA 1976, the Moisture Content of Ghee should not be more than......

a) 0.5%

b) 0.6%

c) 0.8%

d) 0.7%

122) Percentage Fat Recovery in Ghee Prepared by Desi Method is.....

a) 55-65

b) 80-85

c) 75-85

d) 90-95

123) Freezing Point of Fresh Milk is.....

a) -0.54^0C

b) -0.38^0C

c) -0.10^0C

d) 1.2^0C

124) Red Rot in Egg is caused by......

a) *Serratia marcescens*

b) *Pseudomonas putida*

c) *Enterobactor*

d) *Flavobacterium ctyophaga*

125) Yellow Rot in Egg is caused by.....

a) *Serratia marcescens*

b) *Pseudomonas putida*

c) *Enterobactor*

d) *Flavobacterium ctyophaga*

126) Which of the Following in Eggs act as Bacterial Filter Due to Fibrous Nature of Protein?

a) Shell

b) Shell membrane

c) Albumin

d) Yolk

127) Avidin Present in Egg Albumin Binds with......

a) Riboflavin

b) Biotin

c) Thiamin

d) Thiamine

128) Milk Fat Gives Energy around...... C/g.

a) 9.3

b) 4.1

c) 5.2

d) 3.8

129) Milk is Rich in Vitamins except…….

a) A
b) D
c) C
d) E

130) Normal Sizes of Milk fat Globules are…….

a) 2-5μ
b) 10-20 μ
c) 10-12 μ
d) 15-20 μ

131) Meat is Rich in Minerals except…..

a) Iron
b) Copper
c) Iodine
d) All of the above

132) The Carotinoid Content of Buffalo Milk is…… Than Cow Milk.

a) Higher
b) Lower
c) Equal
d) Any of the above

133) Developed or Real Acidity is Due to…….. Formed Bacterial Action on Lactose in Milk.

a) Amides
b) Lactic acid
c) Ammonia
d) Hexonic acid

134) The Following Considerations Involved in Formulation of Standards of Pasteurization are…..

a) Phosphate inactivation
b) Destruction of mycobacterium tuberculosis
c) Cream line reduction
d) All of the above

135) The Time Temperature Combination of HTST Pasteurization of Milk is…..

a) 72^0C for 30 seconds

b) 71^0C for 15 seconds

c) 65^0C for 15 minutes

d) Any of the above

136) The Normal Pressure Maintained in HTST System for Pasteurized Milk is….. PSI.

a) 15

b) 14

c) 13

d) 16

137) Light and Dark Bands are Seen in……

a) Skeletal muscle

b) Smooth muscle

c) Cardiac muscle

d) Both a and b

138) I Band is Bisected by……

a) Z disc

b) Actin

c) Myosin

d) t tubules

139) The Calpins are Calcium Dependent Enzymes, They have a Specific Inhibitor……

a) Calcium ions

b) Calpastatin

c) Cathepstatin

d) Cathepsin

140) The……. of a Color is an Indication of Overall Light Reflectance (Brightness) of The Color.

a) Value

b) Chroma

c) Intensity

d) Hue

141) An Emulsifying Agent Functions to Reduce……..

a) Surface tension
b) Interfacial tension
c) Homogenization
d) Friction

142) …….Are Those Non Meat Materials that Contribute to Both Water Binding and Fat Emulsification Properties.

a) Binder
b) Spices
c) Extendor
d) Filler

143) Those Non Meat Materials Which are able to Bind Large Amount of Water but Contribute Little to Emulsification…..

a) Filler
b) Condiments
c) Binder
d) Extendor

Answers

1.b, 2.b, 3.a, 4.a, 5.c, 6.a, 7.b, 8.a, 9.c, 10.c, 11.c, 12.A, 13.c, 14.a, 15.c, 16.a, 17.a, 18.c, 19.d, 20.b, 21.a, 22.A, 23.a, 24.a, 25.b, 26.c, 27.a, 28.c, 29.a, 30.a, 31.a, 32.C, 33.b, 34.c, 35.a, 36.a, 37.a, 38.b, 39.a, 40.b, 41.d, 42.C, 43.a, 44.c, 45.c, 46.b, 47.a, 48.d, 49.b, 50.b, 51.b, 52.B, 53.b, 54.b, 55.a, 56.a, 57.d, 58.b, 59.c, 60.b, 61.d, 62.A, 63.b, 64.b, 65.b, 66.b, 67.a, 68.b, 69.a, 70.c, 71.a, 72.A, 73.b, 74.a, 75.a, 76.a, 77.a, 78.c, 79.a, 80.b, 81.b, 82.A, 83.d, 84.a, 85.a, 86.a, 87.c, 88.b, 89.b, 90.a, 91.a, 92.B, 93.b, 94.b, 95.a, 96.a, 97.a, 98.d, 99.a, 100.d, 101.a, 102.B, 103.d, 104.a, 105.d, 106.d, 107.a, 108.a, 109.a, 110.a, 111.a, 112.A, 113.a, 114.b, 115.b, 116.d, 117.a, 118.a, 119.a, 120.a, 121.a, 122.B, 123.a, 124.a, 125.d, 126.b, 127.b, 128.a, 129.c, 130.a, 131.d, 132.C, 133.b, 134.d 135.b, 136.a, 137.d, 138.a, 139.b, 140.a, 141.B, 142.a, 143.a.

Chapter - 6

Veterinary Physiology

Dr. Prasanta Kumar K Mishra and Dr. Jatin Kumar Sahoo

1) **Plasma Constitute…… % of the Total Blood**
   a) 55- 65
   b) 80
   c) 45
   d) 35
2) **Arterial Blood is ……as Compare to Venous Blood**
   a) Alkaline
   b) Neutral
   c) Acidic
   d) Highly acidic
3) **Brief Period of Muscular Inactivity Between Two Muscular Twitch**
   a) Response period
   b) Refractory period
   c) Inactivity period
   d) None
4) **Muscle Fibre Length is Directly Related to the Energy of Contraction Explained by**
   a) Steering law
   b) Sterling law
   c) Newton's law
   d) None
5) **Isometric Contraction ……Length of Muscle**
   a) Retains
   b) Retracts
   c) Relaxes
   d) reverses

6) Flat RBC is a Characteristics of

a) Goat
b) Chicks
c) Camel
d) Amphibians

7) Elliptical and Nucleated RBCs are Characteristics of

a) Birds
b) Amphibians
c) Frogs
d) All

8) Hb can bind to CO ……Times more than O_2.

a) 20
b) 890
c) 200
d) Cannot bind

9) Each Gram of Hb Can Carry ……ml of O_2.

a) 1.34
b) 8.9
c) 20
d) 87

10) Graveyard of RBC is

a) Spleen
b) Bone marrow
c) Both a and b
d) Liver

11) Brain Phagocytes are Known as

a) Microglial cells/astrocytes
b) Histiocytes
c) Kupfer cells
d) Monocytes

12) Monocytes Live for Around……

a) 20 minutes
b) A day
c) 200 seconds
d) A week

13) Blood Colloidal Pressure is Mostly Maintained by

a) Bilirubin
b) Albumin
c) Ferritin
d) Alpha-1-anti trypsin

14) Clotting Factor IV is…… and 11 is……

a) Ca and thromboplastin
b) Se and glutathione
c) Pro-convertin and fibrinogen
d) None

15) Basophils Produces……

a) Heparin
b) Melatonin
c) Histamine
d) Epinephrine

16) Dogs Possesses…… Blood Groups

a) 8
b) 9
c) 10
d) 4

17) Cattle have…… Blood Groups

a) 19
b) 8
c) 11
d) 15

18) Heart Rate is Controlled by

a) AV node
b) Valves
c) SA node
d) Aorta

19) Purkinje Fibre are...... Transmitter.

a) Low velocity
b) High velocity
c) Interrupted
d) Irregular

20) Volume of Blood Ejected from Left or Right Ventricle Per Minute

a) Cardiac sufficiency
b) Cardiac strength
c) Cardiac volume
d) Cardiac output

21) Dub Sound is a Result of

a) Closure of AV valve
b) Opening of AV valve
c) Opening of pulmonary valve
d) Closure of pulmonary valve

22) Blood Pressure in Dogs is Commonly Measured From-Artery

a) Femoral
b) Brachial
c) Cervical
d) Tibial

23) Gas Exchange Site is

a) Valves
b) Alveoli
c) Bronchi
d) Bronchiole

24) Respiratory Alkalosis may be Resulted Due to

a) Hypo ventilation
b) Hyper ventilation
c) Acidic inhalation
d) None

25) Expiration Requires……

a) Energy
b) No energy
c) Lot of ATP
d) Heat

26) ……Indicates the Air Breathed During a Normal Respiration

a) Widal volume
b) Tiny volume
c) Tidal volume
d) Total volume

27) The Volume of Gas Remained in Lungs after a Forceful Expiration is known as

a) Remained volum
b) Residual volume
c) Relapsed volume
d) None

28) Chloride Shift also is Designated as

a) Left shift
b) Right shift
c) Hamburger shift
d) Haldane effect

29) To Determine the Haematocr it Value of Blood Which Tube is Being used

a) Wintrobes
b) Neubauer's
c) Mc Caine
d) Kunkel

30) Venous Blood has Partial Pressure of Carbon Dioxide of...... mm Hg

a) 35

b) 85

c) 25

d) 45

31) Dissociation of CO_2 from Hb Post O2 Binding is explained by......

a) Haldane effect

b) Bohrs effect

c) Turners effect

d) None

32) Peripheral Chemoreceptor area are Located in...... and......

a) Carotid and medulla

b) Aortic body and medulla

c) Hypothalamus

d) Carotid body and aortic body

33) Day Night Variation in Physiology of Animal is termed as......

a) Day night variation

b) Circadian rhythm

c) Continuation

d) Adaptation

34) ......is the Most Common Excitatory Neurotransmitter in Peripheral Nervous System

a) Acetylcholine

b) Serotonin

c) Dopamine

d) All

35) Botulinum toxin Inhibits

a) Release of ATP

b) Release of acetyl choline

c) Release of Ca ions

d) None

36) The muscular spasm (tetany) by increased depolarization duration can be brought by

a) Ach inhibitors

b) Organophosphates

c) Insecticides of certain groups

d) All

37) ……is the Principle behind Estimation of Hb in Blood

a) Acid carbonate formation

b) Acid haematin formation

c) Acid citrate formation

d) None

38) Rh factor incompatibility brings a serious disorder known as

a) Erythroblastosis fetalis

b) Big head disease

c) Monster foetu

d) Sickle cell anaemia

39) Myelin forming Glial Cells in CNS are known as

a) Chondrocytes

b) Dendrocytes

c) Oligodendrocytes

d) None

40) Release of Neurotransmitter in Neuromuscular Junctions need Influx of……

a) Na

b) K

c) Ca

d) P

41) Endorphins and Enkephalin…… Pain Sensation

a) Decreases

b) Increases

c) Have other function

d) Does not affect

42) Olfactory Sensation is Processed in

a) Hippocampus

b) Rhinencephalon

c) Prosencephalon

d) Mesencephalon

43) ......is a Mechanism that Directly Regulates a Bodily Function

a) Reflexes

b) Reaction

c) Reflux

d) Repetition

44) The Semi-Circular Organs and Otoliths are Responsible for......

a) Balancing

b) Baroreception

c) Chemoreception

d) Thermoreception

45) The Variable Refraction by Lens makes it Possible to See Clearly at Different Distances by a Process......

a) Adjustment

b) Accommodation

c) Recording

d) Retracting

46) Visual Streaks in the Eye is a Characteristic Feature of

a) Cattle

b) Horse

c) Both a and b

d) Pigs

47) Pineal Gland Secreted Melatonin Exhibits its Function on......

a) Sleep

b) Walking

c) Food intake

d) Digestion

48) Inhibin is Antagonistic to……

a) Estrogen
b) Progesterone
c) FSH
d) LH

49) Growth of Uterus is Attributed by

a) FSH
b) LH
c) GnRH
d) Relaxin

50) Specific Transporters of Lipid Soluble Hormones are

a) Albumin
b) Transferrin
c) Globulin
d) All

51) ……is the Most Important Regulator of Body Fluid

a) Rennin
b) Angiotensin
c) ANP
d) ADH

52) Prolactin Hormone Secretion is inhibited by……

a) Dopamine
b) Serotonin
c) Melanin
d) Melatonin

53) Growth Hormone Exerts its Effect by

a) IGF-I
b) EGF-I
c) VDRF
d) VEGF

54) Iodination of Tyrosine Molecules of Thyroglobulin is mediated by...

a) Thyroperoxidase

b) Iodinase

c) Oxidases

d) Catalases

55) Zona Fasciculata of Adrenal Gland Secretes......

a) Glucocorticoids

b) Nor epinephrine

c) Sex hormones

d) Mineralocorticoids

56) Smooth Muscle Can Develop a Contractile Force Over......

a) Longer time but slow

b) Longer and fast

c) Longer and pulsatile

d) Shorter

57) Smallest Unit of Myofibril is......

a) Sarconeme

b) Sarcomere

c) Sarcosome

d) sarcolith

58) The Membrane of Sr Near to T Tubules Contains a Ca Channel Known as

a) Rynodine receptor

b) OMP receptor

c) ABC transporter

d) P1 channel

59) A Single Tropomyosin Blocks the Binding Site of...... Act in Molecules.

a) 6-8

b) 2-3

c) 15-17

d) 50-60

60) During Prolong Work...... is the Energy Source of Muscle

a) Protein
b) Carbohydrate
c) Fat
d) Amino acids

61) AV Node has Lower Action Potential Due to

a) Leaky Ca channel
b) Leaky Na channel
c) Leaky potassium channel
d) None

62) QRS Complex of ECG Represents

a) Ventricular depolarization
b) Ventricular repolarization
c) Atrial depolarization
d) AV nodal sound

63) TP Interval Indicates

a) Resting heart muscle
b) Depolarized muscles
c) Flaccid Tone
d) Turgid muscle

64) Heart Rate × Stroke Volume =

a) Cardiac strength
b) Cardiac output
c) Cardiac insufficiency
d) None

65) Heart Rate of Mice is...... And Cows...... Beats Per Minute

a) 600-900 and 60-70
b) 60-70 and 600-900
c) 72 and 86
d) 70-100 and 80-120

66) Deficiency of Oxygen Supply to Cells is Known as

a) Anoxia
b) Anorexia
c) Hypoxia
d) axia

67) In a Resting Bird Both Inspiration and Expiration are

a) Passive
b) Active
c) Both
d) None

68) In Eggs…… Forms as Respiratory Organ

a) Shell
b) Allantoin
c) Yolk
d) Chorioallantois

69) The Urine Producing Units in Kidney are

a) Nephron
b) JG apparatus
c) Pelvis
d) Bowman's capsule

70) Kidney Receives…… % of Total Cardiac Output

a) 10
b) 20
c) 80
d) 8

71) Creatinine Excreted in Urine Per Minute Plasma Concentration of Creatinine = ————

a) RGP
b) GGF
c) GFR
d) TFR

72) Glucose and Na Can be Transported by

a) Secondary active transport

b) Primary transport

c) Tertiary transport

d) None

73) Primary Active Secretion in Kidney is Confined to

a) Proximal tubules

b) Loop of Henle

c) Distal tubules

d) None

74) The Lowest Plasma Concentration at which Glucose can be Detected in Urine is known as

a) Renal threshold

b) Maximum range

c) High point

d) Low point

75) Na Absorption is Maximum in Which Part of Kidney

a) Proximal tubules

b) Distal tubules

c) Loop

d) Same for all

76) Urinary Excretion of Na is Highly Regulated by

a) Glucagon

b) Aldosterone

c) Insulin

d) ADH

77) ……Contributes Maximum to the Osmolarity of Urine

a) Creatinine

b) Albumin

c) Glucose

d) Urea

78) Na^{+}, K^{+} and Cl^{-} are ……Pumped Out From Ascending Loop of Henle

a) Actively
b) Passively
c) Both ways
d) Unknown

79) Aldosterone Secretion is stimulated by……

a) Renin
b) Rennin
c) Angiotensin II
d) Angiotensin I

80) ANP from Atrial Muscle Senses

a) Lowered Na^{+} concentration
b) Increased Na^{+} concentration
c) Lowered K^{+} concentration
d) Lowered Ca^{+} concentration

81) Microbial Degradation in the Absence of Oxygen is Known as

a) Rumination
b) Digestion
c) Fermentation
d) Regurgitation

82) BMR/Mass Unit Increases with …….Body Size

a) Increase
b) Decrease
c) Not related
d) None

83) Gastrin is Produced in

a) Oesophagus
b) Cranial part of stomach
c) Caudal part of stomach
d) None

84) Secretin Stimulates Production of HCO_3^- in……

a) Rumen
b) Liver
c) Pancreas
d) Intestine

85) CCK is produced in……

a) Pancreas
b) Liver
c) Duodenum
d) None

86) GIP Reduces Production of……

a) HCO_3^-
b) Insulin
c) Angiotensin II
d) Angiotensin I

87) Satiety and Appetite Centre are located in……

a) Medulla
b) Pons
c) Cerebrum
d) Hypothalamus

88) Leptin are Released From……

a) Fat cells
b) Epithelial cells
c) Retinocytes
d) Myocytes

89) Dental Formula of Horse

a) 3133
b) 2122
c) 0033
d) 1233

90) The Mucus in Saliva Facilitates

a) Chewing
b) Swallowing
c) Tasting
d) Both a and b

91) Salivary Bicarbonate Neutralizes……

a) Bacteria generated acidity
b) Fungus generated alkalinity
c) Soap formation (d) all

92) Forestomach of Ruminant is not used during…… Post Natal Period.

a) 2-3 months
b) 2-3 days
c) 2-3 years
d) 2-3 weeks

93) The Tissues of Forestomach Produces Enzyme……

a) Trypsin
b) Lipase
c) Peptidases
d) None

94) ……Produces Progesterone

a) Corpous luteum
b) Placenta
c) Adrenal medulla
d) All

95) ……Regulates Secretion of FSH and LH

a) PRH
b) GHRH
c) GnRH
d) GGH

96) The GnRH Producing Neurons are gathered in Hypothalamus in....

a) Tonic centre
b) Surge centre
c) Flaccid centre
d) Both a and b

97) Blood Testes Barrier Separates

a) Spermatozoa from blood
b) Spermatozoa from intestinal fluid
c) None
d) Both a and b

98) ATP in Sperm is Produced Mostly in

a) Middle piece
b) Acrosome
c) Tail piece
d) Head

99) Secretion of GnRH, FSH and LH are......

a) Continuous
b) Pulsatile
c) At once
d) Slower

100) During Follicular Phase......

a) Egg matures
b) Ovulation occurs
c) Estradiol is the dominant hormone
d) All

101) During Luteal Phase......

a) Starts embryo development
b) Progesterone released from CL
c) None
d) Both a and b

102) During Follicular Development Some Follicles Stops Growing and Undergo Involution Known as

a) Atresia

b) Degeneration

c) Activation

d) Both a and b

103) Follicular Fluids are Collected in

a) Antrum

b) Gatrum

c) Fulcrum

d) Both a and b

104) The Dominant Follicle Matures to

a) Ovulatory follicle

b) Graafian follicle

c) Secondary follicle

d) Both a and b

105) Length of Estrus in Cow is

a) 15 hours

b) 12 hours

c) 18 hours

d) 28 hours

106) ......The Following is a Short Day Breeder

a) Sheep

b) Goats

c) Deer

d) All

Answers

1.a, 2.a, 3.b, 4.b, 5.b, 6.a, 7.b, 8.c, 9.c, 10.c, 11.a, 12.b, 13.c, 14.c, 15.c, 16.a, 17.c, 18.c, 19.c, 20.d, 21.d, 22.a, 23.b, 24.b, 25.b, 26.c, 27.b, 28.c, 29.b, 30.d, 31.a, 32.b, 33.b, 34.a, 35.b, 36.d, 37.b, 38.a, 39.c, 40.c, 41.a, 42.b, 43.a, 44.b, 45.b, 46.c, 47.a, 48.b, 49.d, 50.b, 51.b, 52.a, 53.a, 54.a, 55a, 56.a, 57.b, 58.b, 59.a, 60.c, 61.b, 62.a, 63.a, 64.b, 65.a, 66.c, 67.b, 68.d, 69.a, 70.b, 71.c, 72.b, 73.a, 74.a, 75.b, 76.b, 77.d, 78.a, 79.c, 80.b, 81.c, 82.b, 83.c, 84.c, 85.c, 86.c, 87.d, 88.a, 89.a, 90.d, 91.a, 92.c, 93.d, 94.d, 95.c, 96.d, 97.b, 98.a, 99.b, 100.d, 101.d, 102.a, 103.d, 104.d, 105.c, 106.d

Chapter - 7

Livestock Production Management

Dr. Sadhna Ojha and Dr. Anupama Jena

1) **Flushing in Sheep is done (When?)**
   a) 2-3 weeks prior to onset of breeding season
   b) After lamning
   c) At the time of breeding
   d) At late pregnancy

2) **Sow which has Conceived for the First Time**
   a) Gilt
   b) Sow
   c) Closed gilt
   d) Open gilt

3) **Jersey of Goat Breed**
   a) Anglo nubain
   b) Angora
   c) Togenberg
   d) Sannen

4) **New Zealand White is a Breed of**
   a) Buffalo
   b) Deer
   c) Rabbit
   d) Sheep

5) **Colt Term Related to which Animal……**
   a) Cattle
   b) Sheep
   c) Buffalo
   d) Horse

6) Chokla is a Breed of

a) Carpet wool breed
b) Fine wool breed
c) Coarse wool breed
d) None of the above

7) Shearing a Term Related to which Animal……

a) Sheep
b) Cattle
c) Yak
d) Buffalo

8) The Smallest Piglet Born in a Litter

a) Runt
b) Gilt
c) Stag
d) None of the above

9) The Act of Giving Birth in Rabbit Called……

a) Kindling
b) Kittenig
c) Kidding
d) Queening

10) The Act of Giving Birth in Goat

a) Kidding
b) Kittenig
c) Kinding
d) Queening

11) Zoological Name of Chicken

a) Numitida meleagridis
b) Gallus Domesticus
c) Meleagridis gallopava
d) None of the above

12) Zoological Name of Horse

a) Equas cabalu
b) Equinus asinus
c) Both of the above
d) None of the above

13) Zoological Name of Buffalo

a) Bos Tauraus
b) Bis Indicus
c) Bubalus Bubalis
d) Equas Cabalus

14) The Act Mating in Case of Pig

a) Tupping
b) Couplin
c) Serving
d) Coverinng

15) The Act Mating in Case of Cattle

a) Tupping
b) Coupling
c) Serving
d) Coverinng

16) The Act Mating in Case of Sheep

a) Tupping
b) Coupling
c) Serving
d) Coverinng

17) The Act of Giving Birth in Case of Sheep

a) Kidding
b) Whelping
c) Lambing
d) Kindling

18) The Act of Giving Birth in Case of Dog

a) Kidding
b) Whelping
c) Lambin
d) Kindling

19) Gestation Period of Pig

a) 100 days
b) 150 days
c) 114 days
d) 90 days

20) Gestation Period of Sheep

a) 100 days
b) 150 days
c) 114 days
d) 90 days

21) Buffalo Breed Which Have Sickle Shape Horn

a) Murrah
b) Mehsana
c) Surti
d) Nilli-Ravi

22) Piglet Should be Given Iron Injection After

a) 4weeks
b) 3 days
c) 4 month
d) 3 weeks

23) Piglet Mortality is Mainly Due to

a) Piglet anaemia
b) Cannibalism
c) Enteritis
d) Crushing by mother

24) Chegu and Changthnagi Goats Produces......

a) Mohair
b) Pushmina
c) Coarse wool
d) None of the above

25) Popular Milch Breed of Cattle in India

a) Tharparkar
b) Sahiwal
c) Ongole
d) Hryana

26) Tallest Goat Breed of Indian Origin

a) Sirohi
b) Marwri
c) Jamunapari
d) None of the above

27) The Best Method of Carcass Disposal is

a) Incineration
b) Surface burning
c) Burial
d) All of the above

28) Castrated Sheep is known as......

a) Buck
b) Wedder
c) Barrow
d) None of the above

29) The Right Method of Milking......

a) Stripping
b) Knuckling
c) Full hand milking
d) None of the above

30) First Feaces Produces from a New Norn Calf is known as……

a) Mucine

b) Feaces

c) Muconium

d) Muconium

31) Best Time for Heat Detection is……

a) Early morning

b) Late evening

c) Both of the above

d) None of the above

32) Mandya Breed of Sheep is Famous for Which Purpose……

a) Wool

b) Meat

c) Milk

d) Milk and meat both

33) Origin of Holstein Friesian is

a) England

b) New Zealnad

c) Holland

d) None of the above

34) Group of Fishes are……

a) School

b) Packs

c) Herd

d) Muster

35) A Ram Castrated after Service is Called Known as……

a) Gimmer

b) Seggy

c) Barren

d) None of the above

36) Essential for New Born Calf is……

a) Colostrum
b) Milk
c) Vitamin supplement
d) None of the above

37) Sheep in which all the Teeth are missing known as..

a) Broken mouth
b) Full mouth
c) Gummer
d) Mature sheep

38) A Group of Cattle Known as……

a) School
b) Troop
c) Herd
d) Pack

39) Dipping is done for……

a) Removal of external parasite
b) Remove bacterial infection
c) Contron internal parasite
d) None of the above

40) Kemp Fibres are……

a) Medullated and discontinuously growing fibre
b) Long and non medullated
c) Very fine fibre
d) Long and dmedullated

41) Cross of Tauras Bulls with Local Cows Known as……

a) Taylor
b) Sunandini
c) Jersind
d) None of the above

42) Cross of Indigenous Breed with Exotic Breed Known as……

a) Taylor

b) Sunandini

c) Jersind

d) None of the above

43) Cross of American Brown Swiss Bulls with Sahiwal and Red Sindhi Known as……

a) Taylor

b) Sunandini

c) Jersind

d) Karan swiss

44) Cross of Tharparkar and Holstein Friesan Known as…

a) Taylor

b) Sunandini

c) Karan fries

d) Karan swiss

45) Cross of Brown Swiss Bull with Local Nondescript Cows Known as……

a) Taylor

b) Sunandini

c) Karan fries

d) Karan swiss

46) Cross of Sahiwal and Holstein Friesan known as……

a) Taylor

b) Sunandini

c) Karan fries

d) Frieswal

47) Canary Coloration is Common in Which Sheep Breed

a) Nali

b) Bhakarwal

c) Angora

d) None of the above

48) Long Staple Fine Wool Known as......

a) Delain wool
b) Dead wool
c) Cotted wool
d) None of the above

49) Wool with Fiber Felting Together due to Lack of Greese in Wool is known as...

a) Delain wool
b) Dead wool
c) Cotted wool
d) None of the above

50) Farrowing Pen with Guard Rail is Essential for......

a) Avoid crushing of piglets
b) Avoid outbreak of disease
c) Avoid crowding
d) None of the above

51) The Primary Purpose of Maintain the Zoo is......

a) Conservatio
b) Recreation
c) Both of the above
d) None of the above

52) Red Data Books Keeps the Details of......

a) Endangered animals
b) Extinct animals
c) Imported animals
d) All of the above

53) The Annual Culling Rate in Dairy Unit is......

a) 25%
b) 45%
c) 55%
d) 65%

54) The Operation Flood "Phase I"……

a) 1960-1965
b) 1965-1970
c) 1970-1975
d) 1975-1980

55) Lnadrace is Breed of……

a) Pig
b) Cattle
c) Horse
d) Rabit

56) Floor Space Required For Dairy Cattle in Case of Intensive System……

a) $4.5m^2$
b) $3.5\ m^2$
c) $5.5\ m^2$
d) $6.5\ m^2$

57) In Laboratory Animals, Male Induced Abortion is known as……

a) Bruce effect
b) Whitten effect
c) Morgan's Effect
d) None of the above

58) Floor Space Required For an Ewe is

a) $2\ m^2$
b) $2.5\ m^2$
c) $1m^2$
d) $0.5\ m^2$

59) Cattle were First Domesticated in

a) Western asia
b) Northern Europe
c) South Africa
d) Leptobos

60) National Dairy Development Board was made in……

a) 1965
b) 1945
c) 1955
d) 1945

61) Indubrasil is a Cross of……

a) Sindhi and Kankrej
b) Gir and kankrej
c) Haryana and kankrej
d) Tharparkar and haryana

62) A Teasure Bull is a……

a) Vasectomised male
b) Uncastrated male
c) Cryptorchid male
d) None of the above

63) The Quantity of Colostrums to be Fed…… of Body Weight of Calf

a) 5%
b) 15%
c) 10%
d) 20%

64) Exotic Breed Which Produces Fine Wool is……

a) Dorset
b) Merino
c) Lincon
d) Dorset

65) Sheep Breed Which Producing Pelt is……

a) Merino
b) Karakul
c) Ramboulliet
d) None of the above

66) Hairs of Angora Breed are known as......

a) Pahmina
b) Kemp
c) Mohair
d) Wool

67) Classification of Buffalo Based on......

a) Milch/meat
b) Water/Swamp
c) Dual
d) None of the above

68) Cattle Breed of India which is known for Powerful Work......

a) Gaolao
b) Rathi
c) Hariyana
d) None of the above

69) For Better Conception a Cow can be inseminated......

a) Standing heat
b) Early heat
c) Late heat
d) After end of oestrus

70) The Bloodless Method of Castration is......

a) Burdizoo
b) Surgical
c) Both of the above
d) None of the above

71) Centre for Karakul Production Located at......

a) Aviakanagar
b) Bikaer
c) Karnal
d) Jaipur

72) Joria is Obtained from which Breed of Sheep

a) Kathiawari

b) Angora

c) Nali sheep

d) None of the above

73) Loi is Obtained from which Breed of Sheep

a) Kathiawari

b) Angora

c) Nali sheep

d) Bhakarwal

74) Black Bengal Goat is Famous for……

a) Mohair

b) Pashmina

c) Glossy Kid skin

d) Nine of the above

75) Canabalism Tendency Seen in which Animal.

a) Hamster

b) Mice

c) Rabbit

d) None if the above

76) Jersey of Goat Breed……

a) Sannen

b) Marwari

c) Jamunapari

d) Nubain

77) Goat Breed which Produces Meat, Milk and Hair……

a) Marwari

b) Sanne

c) Nubain

d) All of the above

78) Yeld/Eild/Barren Related to……

a) An old ewe

b) A lamb not claimed by its mother

c) A ram castrated after service

d) None of the above

79) Which System of Mating is most Common in Commercial Farm

a) Hand service

b) Artificial insemination

c) Flock system

d) None of the above

80) To Prevent Wool Blindness, Excess Wool around the Eyes Should Be clipped regularly, the Process known as……

a) Eyeing

b) Ringing

c) Tagging

d) All of the above

81) Dehornig of Calf Done by Which Method

a) Clipping by saw

b) Cliiping by rubber banf

c) By chemical or electrical method

d) None of the above

82) Permanent Dental Formula of Ruminant is.

a) 3030/3030

b) 0033/4033

c) 0030/4030

d) 3130/3130

83) Best Time for Castration of Pig is……

a) 1 week

b) 2week

c) 4-6 week

d) 8-12 week

84) Best Time for Castration of Calf is……

a) 2 week

b) 1 week

c) 4-6 week

d) 8-10 week

85) Best Time for Castration of Lamb is……

a) 2 week

b) 1 week

c) 4-6 week

d) 8-10 week

86) At Which Time Calf Should Dehorn……

a) Before 10 days old

b) Before 3 days old

c) Before 4 days old

d) Before 5 days old

87) Whole Milk should be Fed at……

a) 9 weeks of age

b) 2 weeks of age

c) 3 weeks of age

d) 5 weeks of age

88) Which Animal Show Standing Heat

a) Cow

b) Pig

c) Sheep

d) Goat

89) Test which is used for Detecting Sow in Heat……

a) Riding test

b) Dye test

c) Hot test

d) None of the above

90) Smallest PIG of a Litter Last to be farrowed……

a) Barrow

b) Runt

c) Crit

d) None of the above

91) Gestation Period of Raabit

a) 1 month

b) 3 week

c) 2 month

d) None of the above

92) Gestation Period of mice

a) 1 month

b) 3 week

c) 2 month

d) None of the above

93) Gestation Period of Guinea Pig

a) 1 month

b) 3 week

c) 2 month

d) None of the above

94) Zoological Name of Guinea Pig…

a) Cavia Porcellus

b) Mesocricetus auratus

c) Rattus Norvegicus

d) Mus musculus

95) Zoological Name of Hamster…

a) Cavia Porcellus

b) Mesocricetus auratus

c) Rattus Norvegicus

d) Mus musculus

96) Zoological Name of Rat (Norvegian)…

a) Cavia Porcellus
b) Mesocricetus auratus
c) Rattus Norvegicus
d) Mus musculus

97) Zoological Name of Mice…

a) Cavia Porcellus
b) Mesocricetus auratus
c) Rattus Norvegicus
d) Mus musculus

98) Which Animal is Pseudoruminant…

a) Camel
b) Sheep
c) Elephnat
d) Deer

99) Highest Dwelling Ruminant in World is…

a) Camel
b) Yak
c) Elephnat
d) Deer

100) Gestation Period of Elephant is…

a) 21-22 month
b) 11-12 month
c) 16-22 month
d) None of the above

Answers

1.a, 2.c, 3.a, 4.c, 5.d, 6.a, 7.a, 8.a, 9.a, 10.A, 11.b, 12.a, 13.c, 14.b, 15.c, 16.c, 17.c, 18.b, 19.c, 20.B, 21.c, 22.b, 23.d, 24.b, 25.b, 26.c, 27.c, 28.b, 29.c, 30.D, 31.a, 32.b, 33.c, 34.a, 35.b, 36.a, 37.c, 38.c, 39.a, 40.A, 41.a, 42.c, 43.d, 44.c, 45.b, 46.d, 47.a, 48.a, 49.c, 50.a, 51.a, 52.a, 53.a, 54.a, 55.a, 56.b, 57.a, 58.c, 59.a, 60.a, 61.b, 62.a, 63.c, 64.b, 65.b, 66.c, 67.b, 68.c, 69.a, 70.a, 71.a, 72.a, 73.d, 74.c, 75.c, 76.c, 77.a, 78.a, 79.b, 80.a, 81.c, 82.b, 83.b, 84.d, 85.a, 86.a, 87.b, 88.b, 89.a, 90.c, 91.a, 92.b, 93.c, 94.a, 95.b, 96.c, 97.d, 98.a, 99.b, 100.a.

Chapter - 8

Animal Genetics and Breeding

Dr. Anupama Jena and Dr. Sadhna Ojha

1) Bouquet Configuration of Chromosome in Which Stage of Cell Division?

a) Telophase

b) Leptotene

c) Pachytene

d) Metaphase-I

2) Zipper like Fashion of Chromosome in Which Stage of Cell Division?

a) Leptotene

b) Zygotene

c) Pachytene

d) Diplotene

3) In the Dark Band of Polytene Chromosome Concentration of ....is More

a) DNA

b) Nucleoprotein

c) Both

d) None of the above

4) Lampbrush Chromosome is Present in...........

a) Salivary gland of drosophila

b) Kuffer cells

c) Amphibian oocyte

d) None of the above

5) Metacentric Chromosome Assumes...... Shape?

a) Y shape
b) U shape
c) L shape
d) V shape

6) Sex Chromosomes are Rich in......

a) Euchromatin
b) Heterochromatin
c) Both
d) None of these

7) The Gene Causing Abnormalities is......

a) Clastogene
b) Plasmagenes
c) Both
d) None of the above

8) Down's syndrome is an Example of......

a) Monosomic
b) Nullisomic
c) Trisomic
d) Double trisomic

9) Complete Synaptonemal Complex is seen in Which Stage......

a) Leptotene
b) Zygotene
c) Pachytene
d) Diplotene

10) Cridu-Chat Syndrome is caused by Deletion of Short Arm of...... Pair of Chromosome in Human

a) 2nd
b) 3rd
c) 4th
d) 5th

11) Who Produced World's first Chromosome Map?

a) Muller
b) Wright
c) Robertson
d) Alfred

12) Chronic Granulocytic Leukaemia is Due to Deletion of Certain Gene in...... Pair of Chromosome of Human Being?

a) 18th
b) 20th
c) 21st
d) 22nd

13) Inversion Occurs at One Side of the Arm and it Does Not Include Centromere......

a) Peri-centric inversion
b) Paracentic inversion
c) Both
d) None

14) Which Among the Following is called as Blending Inheritance?

a) Complete dominance
b) Intermediate dominance
c) Codominance
d) Over dominance

15) Haploid-Diploid Type of Sex Determination is seen in......

a) Wasp
b) Drosophila
c) Rat
d) Butterfly

16) Who Coined the Term Genome?

a) Johannsen
b) Stevens
c) Winkler
d) Jacob-Monod

17) Haptoglobulin in Human Being is an Example of……

a) Complete dominance
b) Intermediate dominance
c) Codominance
d) Over dominance

18) Flower Colour in 4'o Clock Plant is an Example of……

a) Complete dominance
b) Intermediate dominance
c) Codominance
d) Over dominance

19) Feather Shank in Poultry is……

a) Dominant epistasis
b) Recessive epistasis
c) Duplicate dominant epistasis
d) Duplicate recessive epistasis

20) In Case of Complete Linkage the Distance Between Linked Genes are

a) Less than 5 CM
b) 10 CM
c) More than 10 CM
d) None of the above

21) Who Among the Following Possess Complete Linkage?

a) Silk worm moth male
b) Silk worm moth female
c) Drosophila female
d) None of the above

22) Number of chromosome in Yak?

a) 50
b) 54
c) 58
d) 60

23) Number of Chromosome in Musca Domestica?

a) 8

b) 12

c) 14

d) 22

24) Cytoplasmic Inheritance was Experimentally Proved by……

a) Correns

b) Tschemark

c) Wright

d) Mendel

25) Rho Factor is required for Termination of……

a) Translation

b) Transcription

c) Tranversion

d) None of these

26) Total Number of Barr Bodies in an Individual with Turner's Syndrome

a) 0

b) 1

c) 2

d) None of the above

27) Brown Discovered Nucleus in the Cells of……

a) Tradescantia

b) Drosophilla

c) Wasp

d) BGA

28) Number of Linkage Group in Drosophila……

a) 2

b) 4

c) 6

d) 8

29) Interference Value Ranges between……

a) 0-1

b) -1 to 1

c) 0 to infinity

d) None of the above

30) Every Individual has an Equal Chance to Mate among each other is called as……

a) Probability mating

b) Chance mating

c) Panmixia

d) None of the above

31) ……is the Proportionate Contribution of Offspring to The Next Generation.

a) Fitness

b) Selection

c) Correlation

d) Penetrance

32) Z0-ZZ Signifies for

a) Reptiles

b) Bugas

c) Fishes

d) Moth

33) Which among the Following is not a Sex Linked Marker used in Day Old Sexing?

a) Barring

b) Down colour

c) Feathering

d) None of the above

34) Creeper Tail in Poultry is an Example of……

a) Dominant gene

b) Pleitropy

c) Lethal gene

d) None of the above

35) Tetra-Petra Genes in Drosophila is an Example of……

a) Dominance
b) Lethal
c) Pleitropy
d) Penetrance

36) Feulgen Reaction is Specific for……

a) DNA
b) RNA
c) Mitochondria
d) None of the above

37) Pseudogenes are Non-Functional Due to Defects in……

a) Transcription
b) Translation
c) Splicing
d) All of the above

38) First Transgenic Animal Produced is……

a) Sheep
b) Goat
c) Pig
d) Mice

39) Who Developed DNA Finger Printing?

a) Karry Mullis
b) Southern
c) De Flem
d) Alec Jeffery

40) UAG is……

a) Initiation codon
b) Termination codon
c) Both
d) None of the above

41) Genetic Code is……

a) Universal

b) Degenerate

c) Unambiguous

d) All of the above

42) Beadle and Tautum used Which Organism for Their Study……

a) Drosophila

b) Neurospora

c) Mice

d) None of the above

43) What is Balanced Lethal System?

a) When homozygous dominant survive

b) When homozygous recessive survive

c) When heterozygous survive

d) None of the above true

44) Who Proposed RRS?

a) Robinson

b) Hull

c) Hazel

d) Lush

45) Who Proposed Method of Selection?

a) Robinson

b) Hull

c) Hazel

d) Jerkin

46) Which Exotic Cattle's Milk High in Beta-Carotene?

a) Ayshire

b) Guernsey

c) Jersey

d) None of the above

47) Panchkalyani is the Other Name of which Buffalo Breed?

a) Murrah
b) Surti
c) Jafferbadi
d) Nili-Ravi

48) Roman nose is the Characteristic Feature of......

a) Gaddi
b) Beetal
c) Barbari
d) Jamunapari

49) Largest Sheep Breed of World?

a) Merino
b) Lincoln
c) Romney Marsh
d) Corriedale

50) Mutton Traits have......

a) High heritability
b) Low heritability
c) Medium heritability
d) Cannot say

51) Egg Quality Traits have......

a) High heritability
b) Low heritability
c) Medium heritability
d) Cannot say

52) Fertility and Hatchability both have......

a) High heritability
b) Low heritability
c) Different heritability pattern
d) None of the above

53) Among Full Sib Selection and Half Sib Selection which One is Most Favoured?

a) Full sib selection

b) Half sib selection

c) Both of these

d) None of these

54) Among Full Sib Selection and Half Sib Selection which One is most Accurate?

a) Full sib selection

b) Half sib selection

c) Both of these

d) None of these

55) Between Family Selection is Most Preferred in……

a) C& B

b) Pig

c) Poultry

d) Small ruminants

56) Within Family Selection is Most Preferred in……

a) C & B

b) Pig

c) Poultry

d) Small ruminants

57) $P = P_f + P_w$, if $P_f = 1$ and $P_w = 0$ Then which among the Following selection is Most Preferred?

a) Individual selection

b) Family selection

c) Combined selection

d) Pedigree selection

58) $P = P_f + P_w$, if $P_f = P_w$ Then Which Among the Following Selection is most Preferred

a) Individual selection

b) Family selection

c) Combined selection

d) Pedigree Selection

59) Which Among the Following is called as Dairy Search Index?

a) Corrected Daughter Average Index

b) Contemporary daughter average index

c) Corrected contemporary daughter average index

d) None of the above

60) BLUP Was Developed by……

a) Lush

b) Henderson

c) Robinson

d) None of the above

61) Who Coined the Term Clone?

a) McGrat

b) Haldane

c) Kammath

d) Copier

62) Hardy-Weinberg Law is Applicable to……

a) Autosomal genes

b) Sex linked genes

c) Holandric genes

d) None of the above

63) Who Coined the Term "Genetic Drift"?

a) Lush

b) Henderson

c) Robinson

d) None of the above

64) Genes Contribute Much More Variance When They are at……

a) Intermediate frequency

b) High frequency

c) Low frequency

d) Does not affect

65) ……utilizes Non-Additive Genetic Variance?

a) GCA
b) SCA
c) Both
d) None of the above

66) Which among The Following does not Cause Change in Gene Frequency?

a) Selection
b) Inbreeding
c) Mating system
d) Migration

67) Mildest form of Outbreeding is……

a) Cross breeding
b) Out crossing
c) Species hybridization
d) Rotational breeding

68) Most Effective Method of Selection is……

a) Progeny testing
b) Family selection
c) Individual selection
d) Pedigree Selection

69) Crossing of Two Inbred Lines of the Same Breed is……

a) Incrossing
b) Incross breeding
c) Top crossing
d) Top cross breeding

70) RRS is Used to Improve only……

a) Only GCA
b) Only SCA
c) Both GCA and SCA
d) None of the above

71) Top...... Percentage of Recorded Cows are Elite Cows.

a) 5%

b) 10%

c) 20%

d) 25%

72) Inbred Line is the Result of...... Generations of Full Sib Mating?

a) 2

b) 4

c) 7

d) None of the above

73) Out-Crossing is......

a) Within breed crossing

b) Between breed crossin

c) Both

d) None of the above

74) Beef Master is a Cross Between......

a) Brahman* Shorthorn

b) Brahman * Shorthorn* Hereford

c) Brahman* Hereford

d) None of the above

75) Who gave the Term Homozygous and Heterozygous?

a) Waldeyer

b) Bateson

c) Morgan

d) Hugo de vries

76) Haemophilia is a......

a) Sex-linked inheritance

b) Sex-limited inheritance

c) Sex-influenced inheritance

d) None of these

77) Wobble Hypothesis was proposed by……

a) Beadle and Tautum

b) Waldeyer

c) Morgan

d) Crick

78) Type of gamete in F_2 is……

a) 2^n

b) 3^n

c) 4^n

d) None of the above

79) Father of Modern Animal Breeding……

a) Morgan

b) Bakewell

c) Hull

d) Lush

80) Who Discovered Transduction?

a) Griffith

b) Zinder and Laderberg

c) Laderberg and Tautum

d) None of the above

81) Who Discovered Conjugation?

a) Griffith

b) Zinder and Laderberg

c) Laderberg and Tautum

d) None of the above

82) Hen and Cock Feathering is……

a) Sex-linked inheritance

b) Sex-limited inheritance

c) Sex-influenced inheritance

d) None of these

83) Father of Biostatistics?

a) Galton

b) Gosset

c) Pearson

d) Fisher

84) T Test was developed by……

a) Galton

b) Gosset

c) Pearson

d) Fisher

85) Who Proposed Design of Experiment?

a) Galton

b) Gosset

c) Pearson

d) Fisher

86) Father of Modern Biostatistics?

a) Galton

b) Gosset

c) Pearson

d) Fisher

87) In Normal Distribution……

a) Mean, median, mode coincide

b) Mean > mod

c) Mean < median

d) Cannot say

88) Non-Parametric Equivalent of Two Independent Sample T-test is……

a) Wald-wolfowitz test

b) Mann-whitney U test

c) Fisher's exact probability test

d) None of the above

89) Friedmann's Test is for……

a) One way analysis of ANOVA
b) Two way analysis of ANOVA
c) Both
d) None of the above

90) Range of Multiple Correlation Coeficient is……

a) 0-1
b) -1 to 1
c) 1 to infinity
d) None of the above

91) Level of Significance is Equal to Probability of……

a) Type-I error
b) Type-II error
c) Both
d) None of the above

92) Range of Correlation Coefficient is……

a) 0-1
b) -1 to 1
c) 1 to infinity
d) None of the above

93) Yate's Correction is applied in which Test?

a) Chi square test
b) T-test
c) Z-test
d) None of the above

94) Most Commonly used Method of Central Tendency………

a) Mean
b) Median
c) Mode
d) None of the above

95) Median Falls at……

a) 25th percentile
b) 50th percentile
c) 75th percentile
d) All of the above

96) Measures of Dispersion Influenced by Extreme Values……

a) Range
b) Standard deviation
c) Variance
d) All of the above

97) Rejecting the Null Hypothesis when it is Correct is……

a) Type-I error
b) Type-II error
c) Both
d) None of the above

98) Hypothesis Proposed for Rejection is……

a) Null hypothesis
b) Alternative hypothesis
c) Both
d) All of the above

99) When Each and Every Unit in the Population has an Equal Chance of Selection is……

a) Systematic sampling
b) Cluster sampling
c) Random sampling
d) None of the above

100) Level of Significance is denoted by……

a) α
b) β
c) γ
d) $1-\beta$

Answer

1.b, 2.b, 3.a, 4.c, 5.d, 6.b, 7.a, 8.c, 9.b, 10.d, 11.d, 12.d, 13.b, 14.b, 15.a, 16.c, 17.d, 18.b, 19.d, 20.a, 21.b, 22.d, 23.b, 24.a, 25.b, 26.a, 27.a, 28.b, 29.a, 30.c, 31.a, 32.d, 33.d, 34.c, 35.d, 36.a, 37.d, 38.d, 39.d, 40.b, 41.d, 42.b, 43.c, 44.a, 45.c, 46.b, 47.d, 48.d, 49.b, 50.a, 51.a, 52.b, 53.b, 54.a, 55.c, 56.b, 57.b, 58.a, 59.c, 60.b, 61.b, 62.a, 63.d, 64.a, 65.b, 66.b, 67.b, 68.a, 69.a, 70.c, 71.b, 72.a, 73.a, 74.b, 75.b, 76.a, 77.d, 78.c, 79.d, 80.b, 81.c, 82.c, 83.a, 84.b, 85.d, 86.d, 87.a, 88.b, 89.b, 90.a, 91.a, 92.b, 93.a, 94.a, 95.b, 96.a, 97.a, 98.a, 99.c, 100.a.